THREE'S COMPANY

An unexciting family holiday in Cornwall is trans-
formed when Chris finds himself drawn to an aloof
but attractive local girl, Rowan. Alive as he has
never been before, Chris is soon seeing his family
through new eyes, and becoming increasingly self-
aware as he allows himself to be drawn into the
holiday group. In the company of Rowan and her
vulnerable friend Rose, Chris discovers that his
own ideas about girls are very different from his
experienced brother's and, through his increasing
concern for Rose, he learns the distinction
between love and friendship.

THREE'S COMPANY

Jean MacGibbon

Chatto & Windus

Published by
Chatto & Windus Ltd
40 William IV Street
London WC2N 4DF

*

Clarke, Irwin & Co Ltd
Toronto

British Library Cataloguing in Publication Data

MacGibbon, Jean
    Three's company
    I. Title
    823'.9'1F   PZ7.M16753
    ISBN 0-7011-2295-1

Copyright © Jean MacGibbon 1978
ISBN 0 7011 2295 1

Printed in Great Britain by
R. & R. Clark, Ltd, Edinburgh

For Lucy Cabot

CHAPTER ONE

1959

Chris and Nick Mitchell lay sprawled on their beds in the Cornish holiday cottage, waiting for tea-time, waiting for the fierce afternoon heat to let up, jeans unzipped, shirts open to the waist. When they heard the galloping horse, Nick, propped up on one elbow, was shooting potato pellets at a pin-up girl he had stuck on the wall. She wore jeans, but her top half was naked except for a cowboy hat and a neckerchief, and Nick had pencilled round her tits to look like targets.

At the sound of these hooves drumming on dry turf he sat up. Nick was crazy about Westerns and still kept a fake gun in his sox drawer, though he was nineteen and worked in the Invoicing and Despatch Department in a brewery, and was a never-ending source of surprise and speculation for Chris who was sixteen and still at school.

The hooves, striking gravel, slowed to a trot.

Nick went to the window: 'A girl in a Stetson hat – she's stopping!'

Hooves scraped to a halt. A murmur of voices. Then their mother called up the stairs.

'Chris – come down, will you?'

Chris zipped up his jeans at the head of the crooked staircase. Mrs Mitchell, at the half-open door that was like a stable door, said, 'This is Rowan – Rowan Marsh. Her mother sent a note – remember? – asking you to a dance tonight.'

The girl sat up very straight astride her brown horse with a black mane. Under the broad-brimmed hat her dark hair followed the curve of her cheeks. Unsmiling she said, 'Mum thought you might like to come over to supper before the dance.'

'Yeah. Thanks.' He leant over the half-door and patted the pony's neck. Refusing Mrs Mitchell's offer of tea, she wheeled her pony round, trotted past the terraced cottages till the gravel ended, broke into a canter and cleared a low bank.

'Looking you over, was she?' Nick from the bedroom window blew curls of smoke from a thin black cigar. 'Wise girl – no blind dates for her.'

Chris sat slumped on a bench. He wasn't keen on dates fixed for him by his mother, blind or not. He hadn't much wanted to go to the dance, and seeing the girl didn't make him any keener. He wasn't any good at chatting up girls and she didn't look as though she'd be easy.

He looked across two fields to Oyster Bay and the river which had been blue, but now, because of the sun's angle, had turned leaden, colourless, with steep fields and dark massed trees on the opposite bank. The tide was out so there'd be no chance of a swim until the water crept up and covered the mud-flats once more.

So far the holiday had been a dead loss for Chris. Nick had seen the advert for the cottage and persuaded their parents to book it for a fortnight, though they'd never been in these parts before, because the advert promised sailing. But there had been no wind for sailing until yesterday, when they had all zig-zagged inexpertly down to the mouth of the estuary. His Dad, who fancied himself at the helm, hadn't sailed since boyhood. Nick and he had argued, their mother had shut them up and he, Chris, had been sick.

He was keen on swimming, but not in this land-locked bay where there were no waves and no foreshore to speak of. He liked cycling and had chosen to cycle down from London, stopping at youth hostels. But his bike had been damaged the day of his arrival when he had left it lying in a field while he looked for someone to direct him, halfway along the deserted two-mile track that connected the cottages with the main road. He returned to find some fool of a horse had put its foot through the front wheel spokes.

There wasn't anything he wanted to do. Sixteen was a lousy age, he thought. Fifteen had been so frightful, he had expected things to get better. But sixteen was worse because you were that much older, school work harder swotting for exams, and people were beginning to ask what you intended to do after leaving school.

His mother came out: 'Tea. I wish you wouldn't slop around all day. You might as well be at home.'

Chris refrained from saying that he wished he was, and followed her into the kitchen, which was at first too dark to see anything after the dazzle outside. The uneven stone flags were cool on his bare feet.

Mr Mitchell and Nick were already tucking into splits and cream and raspberry jam.

'You ought to mix more,' his mother pursued. 'The people in the other cottages look a nice crowd, and they always seem to find plenty to do on the beach, fixing up their boats, going fishing. Why aren't you more friendly with them?'

'Because they all know each other,' Nick answered for him. 'Because they've been coming here for years, and call each other funny names like "Tosh" and "Pinky". No, it's true, I've heard them. And "Mog".'

'Mog's a spaniel,' Chris corrected him.

'Tomorrow,' their mother said, 'if there's still no wind for sailing, we'll drive over to the North coast. They have surfing there, with waves coming straight in from the Atlantic. You'd like that?'

'It'd be O.K.' Chris couldn't dredge up enthusiasm for anything, specially with the family crowding in on him. He couldn't breathe properly.

Mr Mitchell shifted, reaching for another split, and his chair creaked. He was heavily built: 'Not on your nelly. I'm not taking the car over that dirt track oftener than I have to. And think of the crowds, in August. We'd never get through those narrow lanes, not all that distance. It was

9

bad enough getting here.'

'I can't stand Chris loafing around. It's not good for his health. And Nick's just as bad. Though you're old enough to please yourself.'

'So's Chris,' Nick retorted, 'old enough to please himself. Trouble with you is that just because you're a physio and go about all day on your toes you think everyone else ought to.' Mrs Mitchell worked in a hospital physiotherapy department.

'I don't understand young people,' she sighed, halfway along a well-known train of complaint. 'You've got all the facilities for sport –'

'Look where sport got me,' her husband intervened. His hairy belly bulged between shirt and trousers. 'O.K., O.K. So it's the beer. I mean to say Chris isn't doing too bad. Going to this Yacht Club dance, aren't you? Wish *I* was!'

'Why don't you go too, Nick? It'd give Chris confidence.'

'For Chrissake! We're on our own now, Chris as well as me. If Chris hasn't got confidence – and I'm not saying he hasn't – it's up to him. Course I wouldn't go pushing in on his evening. It'd be the last thing . . . Besides which, I wasn't asked. That hat . . . Ask the kid where she got it. Not in England, for sure. It's the real McCoy.'

Chris got up, biting into a half-eaten split: 'If you've all finished talking me over, I'll get out.'

Leaning over the open half-front door he saw a string of dinghies spaced out and made fast to a cable which, he had learnt today from Nick, was called a pulley-hauley. He heard the squeak of the block attached to a stout tree as the cable was paid out, allowing the little boats to float in deep water. The pulley-hauley made it possible to land or sail away whatever the state of the tide.

Before long the people from the other cottages began to trail up through the fields, more than a dozen of them, different ages down to small kids, carrying oars, a string of mackerel, a pail of mussels carried by a boy about Chris's age followed by a cocker spaniel. He was taller than Chris, but lightly built, long-limbed, round-shouldered from habitually walking with bent head. His hair, bleached almost to whiteness, needed cutting, and as he took the stone stile in three loping strides a strand fell over his eyes and he tossed his hair back. Those eyes, a blazing blue, were deep-set in his smooth-skinned brown face, and in this, as in other ways, he was so much like the others with him that Chris had come to think of them not so much as one family, or nearly related, as they surely must be, but as a race of beings unlike himself who inhabited the place. He did not want to talk to them but liked to watch them, as he might have watched a herd of roe-deer in a park near his home.

They talked among themselves, passing Chris with friendly, offhand nods. Though the boy with the slopping pail looked as though he might have got into conversation if Chris had been responsive.

But Chris was thinking about the week after next. The fruit-picking camp. Miles away from his family. Last year . . . hot tents, the smell of bruised grass, a girl called Bella. Purple bloomy plums, with him and Bella up the same tree, plum juice round her mouth and down the front of her thin shirt. Laughing, she'd leant forward and kissed him full on the mouth, so quick, so unexpected that he hadn't time to believe it had happened before she had moved, leaning down to lower her basket so that he could see between her breasts, and climbed down.

The last evening, that had been, with a barbecue and dancing to end up. Bella stayed close to her boy-friend and never gave Chris another look, and he hadn't tried approaching her because what would have been the use? She was at least two years older. At fifteen he had been the youngest in the camp.

But the kiss had stayed with him. For a whole year.

CHAPTER TWO

After tea Chris lay on his bed again, watching Nick get ready to go out. He had teamed up with one of the crowd next door because the man had a car and they could drive in to Porthmawgan. From the way he was acting Chris guessed he was dating a girl. Deodorant under his striped shirt that fitted down to the waist and disappeared without trace under hip-hugging jeans so tight round the calves that he could hardly get into them. Nick was the best-looker Chris had ever seen, and most of all he prized his brother's slim hips, the whole line of his long body. After-shave patted into tanned cheeks, faintly scented to match the deodorant. Then the scrutiny for spots in a magnifying shaving mirror. Finally Nick blew into cupped hands, testing for bad breath. This routine fascinated Chris, part of the never-ending dossier he was compiling in his head about his elder brother, facts observed but not always understood. A blueprint for growing up. It puzzled him that a man with Nick's looks and outward assurance, his undoubted knowledge of worldly affairs, should be obsessed with bad breath. And other uncertainties, gestures of indecision, a way of clearing his throat.

Girls could do this to him. This fact, however surprising, had to be fitted in along with the toy revolver and the Western shoot-ups he and his mates went in for during the lunch hour in the loading bay at the factory.

'See ya,' Nick cast an eye over his kid brother. 'You'll do,' he nodded, and clattered down the bare winding stair.

Too hot for a tee-shirt, Nick had fixed him up with a loose, tan shirt that he could open down the front and tie the ends of if it got hotter at the dance. Chris couldn't see himself going this far, but you never knew.

'Well!' his mother exclaimed at the foot of the stairs,

then, not wanting to undermine his confidence: 'Nice and cool,' was the most she could comment.

His Dad remarked, 'A bit tight round the hams, though. Have to watch it, boy, you got my figure, basically.' After a closer look: 'That what they wear at Yacht Clubs these days?' He shrugged: 'If Nick says so.'

Chris knew the two of them were leaning over backwards not to seem "square". But why comment at all? 'We're both on our own now,' Nick had said.

The three of them walked down as far as the bank the girl had jumped on her pony, then his parents branched off, going down to the shore. They were taking the dinghy, with the outboard attached, across to the pub at Trewin village down-river.

Chris continued across a dried-up meadow where some despondent cows were chewing on the little they could get. They looked up; Chris kept going at a steady pace, wanting to run, though he had been told they were just naturally curious, till he reached the shelter of woods that extended to the water's edge, and found a path that led round a promontory.

He knew where the Marshes lived. Garrow Cottage. Mrs Marsh hired out boats, and Nick and their father had gone round the first day to hire *Seamouse*, the sailing dinghy.

The wood was thick with scrub oaks, darker but less cool than the open field. Once round the promontory there was more wind. Through clearings the estuary could be seen, blue and sparkling now, stretching away, widening past rocky headlands and bays to the sea. Tall-masted boats, pleasure craft of every description made the view interesting. He spotted *Seamouse;* they hadn't taken the outboard after all but had hoisted sail. The whole thing was flapping and veering from side to side, out of control. They should have had Nick there; Nick knew how to sail. At least, in theory.

He sat down on a rocky patch of heather projecting over the water, clear blue-green in shadow, savouring the salty breeze, counting the days till the fruit-picking, thinking of Bella.

A twig cracked behind him. Up there on the path stood a girl with light, shoulder-length hair and a dress the colour of shadowed water that hung straight from her shoulders, falling almost to her bare ankles.

'Hullo. You must be Chris. I'm Rose, staying with the Marshes.'

He joined her as she picked her way along the path in bare feet, protecting her dress from brambles, not turning round to speak. Her body under the thin stuff showed its shape as she moved, reminding him of Bella.

She led him to a clearing at the water's edge, a boathouse, six or seven boats on the grass or on moorings. A girl – Rowan – was bending down in one afloat, a sturdy motor-sailer, doing something to the engine. A woman came out of the boathouse, meeting Chris with a welcoming smile. She was big and strong-looking, wearing a checked shirt and rolled-up jeans. Her bare arms were muscular but rounded, and her neck and throat curved smoothly up out of her open shirt; Chris saw at once that she was more like Bella than Rose had seemed. Bella, say, in twenty years' time.

'Damn people took out *Shearwater*, left the propeller fouled and the engine – are you any good with engines? Diesels?'

Chris said no: not diesels.

'We'll get Steve down after supper. From the boatyard. Come on Rowan. Leave the bloody thing.'

Rowan came ashore, nodding briefly to Chris. He helped them clear up and Mrs Marsh led the way up a steep path, Chris carrying a sail that needed mending.

The path led through dense bushes, creepers tangled with purple spiked flowers that attracted Red Admiral butterflies, and saplings that gave off bruised, sappy smells, bittersweet and spicy, sub-tropical, he imagined, brushing midges and spider-threads from his sweaty face.

14

He began to feel alive, expectant, for the first time since his arrival.

They came out on a level stretch of lawn, a table, and beyond, a white thatched cottage.

'Sit down while Rowan changes,' Mrs Marsh suggested. He waited on a bench rough with blistered blue paint, and presently Rose brought out a frosted jug of cider-cup. Ice clinked, there were slivers of peach and mint leaves; the drink was heady, delicious.

'It's stronger than you'd think.' Rose poured a second glass for them both. She had lived in Porthmawgan, she told him, till her family moved away. She and Rowan had been to school together and Rowan used to stay for the night when Danny – Mrs Marsh – worked nights at the hospital. Rowan's father had been killed in the war. Danny was great, wasn't she?

Chris agreed.

There were silences between them, but such was the coolness and strangeness of the place that Chris felt no need to talk. He felt easy, relaxed, and cooking smells through the open door made his tummy rumble.

At supper Rowan appeared after they had finished their melon. Chris noticed her legs as she came slowly down the cottage stairs, long, slim and brown, more shapely than he could have guessed from seeing her in jeans.

'That's a good colour,' her mother commented, 'burnt orange.'

Rowan's full, mid-calf length skirt glowed in the shadowy, stone-walled room, contrasting with her black sleeveless top. Her small waist was cinched in with a wide belt. As she sat down beside him her dark hair, brushed all to one side, fell between them like a curtain; when she spoke to him, which wasn't often, she draped it behind her ear, with a small gold earring in the lobe, and let it fall again. She had dark eyes and full red lips like her mother's.

What talk there was passed between Chris and Mrs Marsh. She was a good listener. He found himself telling her about his family, about his disappointment with sailing, and how some fool of a horse had put his hoof through his bike wheel.

'That was Snapdragon, my pony,' Rowan said coldly. Her mouth had a funny curl to it, and he couldn't be sure if she were altogether angry, or a little amused as well.

'I thought he'd cut himself on barbed wire,' she said when he had apologised. Both girls broke out laughing.

'It sounded so funny,' Rose explained, 'you finding Snapdragon with her foreleg through the spokes.'

No one seemed to consider his damaged bike.

'He wasn't to know,' Mrs Marsh got up. 'You ought to be leaving.'

'The Yacht Club's a snobby place,' Rowan grumbled, 'I don't know why we go.'

'Everyone goes,' Rose said, 'and you don't have to talk to the snobby ones.' She danced a few steps, and in the green light from the deep-set window she looked like a fish in water.

'Mog's gone straight to the Club,' Rose said, 'he's been racing.'

'Mog? Thought he was a spaniel.'

But the two girls had gone on ahead. Chris was thankful they hadn't heard what must have seemed a mad, inexplicable comment.

Mrs Marsh chuckled, seeing his bewildered face. 'You'll get used to it, the way they carry on here. Sixteen years, and the place hasn't changed. Still the same little in-groups, funny talk. Coming from Wyoming, I thought everyone stand-offish or plain crazy. Took me years.'

So that's how Rowan got her hat, thought Chris, remembering to tell Nick.

The three of them slithered barefoot over the weedy, rocky foreshore. Rowan, loosing a painter, hauled in the boat and they climbed aboard. The water was pleasantly warm. She turned the starting handle with impressive ease and steered them down the narrow creek, leaning against

16

the tiller, steering with her body, tall in her full skirt like a figurehead on an old ship.

This, thought Chris, was the kind of boating he could take to, steady and purposeful – going somewhere definite. The stillness which now lay over darkening woods and water might have been depressing on his own, but the girls' company made it all right. More than all right. For Chris, tending to expect the worst, was surprised by enjoyment.

They passed big sailing boats moored in mid-stream for the night, with lighted portholes, smells of cooking, a murmur of voices. Music. A boat big enough to live on – that might be good. Perhaps he would get over being seasick.

A promontory of jagged rocks protected the entrance to the creek from the main channel; once this was rounded they were in full light again, under the immensity of the evening sky that was reflected in water, a harder blue than the sky, a deeper pink lapped in the hollows of the gentle swell.

The Yacht Club, high up above the shore, was lit with coloured lamps. The amplified beat of rock music carried far over the water. The terrace with its low parapet was crowded. A boy detached himself as they mounted the steps; the boy from the cottages who had been carrying the pail of mussels. He smiled in a friendly way when Rose introduced them: 'Mog – this is Chris.'

'I know. Often seen you.' He and Rose turned into the Club bar.

'Like to dance?' Chris asked Rowan after she had responded to a number of greetings with her polite but off-putting smile.

'We could try. I'm not much good.'

They danced for a while in the bar room, too crowded for Rowan's dancing to matter much. True, she moved rather stiffly; but she was the best-looking girl in the room, Chris had decided after a quick survey, and there wasn't anyone he'd rather have been with, he thought, as her brown hand slipped into his, her palm hard and dry in spite of the heat, and he attempted to swing her round. She wasn't quick enough to respond before the small space closed up and the movement was checked. He wanted to know more about her.

The record ended. At the bar they found themselves in a group from the cottages. The high pitch of their voices, the sureness of their chatter, reduced Chris to silence, grateful for Rowan's low, thoughtful, gently mocking replies. She was among friends, and her wide, curly smile showed she felt easy with them. Which prompted Chris to make an effort to join in.

The girl "Tosh" was at his elbow.

'You look awfully alike,' he ventured to comment, glancing at her blue eyes, short upper lip and shining sunbleached hair, 'all you people in Oyster Cottages. Fair. But a few darker ones.'

'We're cousins – three families. We come here in the holidays, it's the only time we're ever all together. The fair ones are Travises, the dark ones Pernels. Mog's my brother, and there are three younger ones. Our father's Jack Travis – everyone calls him Jack – he's not here tonight. Uncle Ben – Ben Pernel – is over there talking to the Commodore. Aunt Jane – that's Uncle Ben's wife – she isn't here either. She's sailing home from Portugal. It's frightfully confusing, I know. And in the end cottage there are more Travises – Dad's younger brother – his lot.'

Rose and Mog joined them. 'They've got a barbecue going outside.'

Chris and Rowan found a place in the corner of the terrace furthest from the barbecue. Neither wanted to eat.

'I shouldn't have worn a skirt,' Rowan gestured towards a girl going past in jeans, 'only Rose was keen to wear her dress. She's just made it from a pattern in an American fashion magazine. A bit weird, isn't it? It's called the "sack", she says. She's keen on fashion – wants to be a dress designer.'

'I like full skirts and tight waists better.'

18

'Rose thinks she's too fat for them. She is, too. But I like the way she looks.'

'Your mother was right about the colour of your skirt. It suits you. Doesn't she ever come to this sort of thing?'

'Not unless she has to. She hates these social get-togethers. So do I, only she makes me come. Always on about me not meeting enough people.'

Chris looked out across the estuary. A star or two had risen above the high ground on the opposite bank. And there were moving lights on the river, boats returning from a cruise, slipping on to their moorings, a light on a mast-head taller than the rest gliding majestically upstream.

'I've never been anywhere like this.'

'There isn't anywhere like it. I couldn't live anywhere else. Nor could Mother. But she thinks I ought to, later on.'

'If I lived here I don't suppose I should want to leave. The only thing is . . .' What he had in mind seemed impossible to explain.

'No jobs, you were going to say? There aren't, not many. Or what?'

'It's too beautiful, the place.'

As Rowan stayed silent, he continued, 'We used to go to the East Coast for holidays. Walton-on-the-Naze, where Dad's aunt lived. It's flat and there's always a wind, with no shelter except behind dykes – that's if you go out of town, the dykes – it's good for cycling, except for the wind, and that's what I mostly did when I was old enough. Got away into the country.'

The little seaside resort was so far away in memory, so totally different from his present surroundings, that it was difficult to recall. What had made them return there year after year? Good for small kids, he supposed, the beach. Cheap to get to – the station within walking distance of his aunt's. Best draught stout anywhere in the station buffet, his Dad used to say.

It was his turn to be silent, ruminating.

'Go on. What's wrong with living here?'

'Sorry.' He stretched his arms and clasped them behind his head. 'That's what I mean. There I felt whipped up into doing things. Here I feel sleepy all the time. If I lived here maybe I couldn't do a job even if there was one.'

'People usually feel sleepy when they first come, but they get over it. Sometimes they stay and don't work. It's easy here to live without – with hardly any money. There was one man came down from London, watched the crabbers go out, stayed on, watched how they made their pots in winter. That he could do. He was good with his hands. He was an artist, well, a sort of artist. In the spring he bought a boat. But of course it was no good.'

'Why?'

'He never got any crabs to speak of, or lobsters. Or dabs. Only mackerel, which anyone can get. He didn't know where to lay his pots, or how, or where the fishing grounds were, and the men weren't telling him.'

'What happened to him?'

'He stuck it out for a year or more. Mother let him have Otter Lodge up Mirren Creek. She and Dad built it them-selves – lived there when they first married. Would you like to see it? We could take a boat up.'

'This man – isn't he here any more? Did he go back to town?' Chris was already picturing himself living in a hut in the woods. Cut off from his family, free from questioning about what he was going to do when he left school. 'What did he live on?'

'Mackerel. The odd rabbit. He knew about wild plants – what you could eat, roots and berries. He worked a bit. Potato-picking – worked for a farmer when there were extra hands needed. Mum cooked him pasties and that. He'd row down and see us, winter nights. He was nice. I was just a kid at the time. He made us things. Wood-carvings. And things made from what he picked up on the beach. Sur-prising what you can find if you have an eye for it. I used to go around with him, beach-combing. But it's not much fun on your own. After Jago left . . .'

Listening to her tone of voice, Chris thought: she fancies the bloke! How could she? This old scrounger (he imagined an unshaven face, bleary eyes) and Rowan – "just a kid" – *how* old?

'When was that? When did he go?'

'Couple of years back. He didn't exactly *leave* . . .' The irony, the edge to her voice, were unmistakable. 'He went to work for Mrs Trewin. She owns all the land this side of the river up as far as Mirren Farm. We don't see Jago any more. Mother and Mrs Trewin don't get on. Nor me neither.'

'Jago? That's another funny name.'

'It's quite common in Cornwall. His real name was Smithers. Mrs Trewin called him Jago. Suits him much better.'

'Mrs Trewin – I fetch the milk from her farm. She and the river – the same name?'

'Her family have lived here – oh, I don't know. Since before the Romans; according to her the river was named after them. *She* says she's descended from a Celtic chieftain.' Rowan giggled. 'Looks like it too. Haven't you seen her?'

'Don't think so.'

'She thinks she owns the river.'

Mog and Rose had come up. 'She thinks she *is* the river,' Mog said, without further elucidation. 'Come and dance, Rowan. Rose wants to dance with Chris. She was watching you.'

Rose caught his hand. 'Idiot!' she looked at Mog with easy affection. Chris was envious: just one girl, he thought longingly. Someone I could talk to and feel easy with. But it would take time. Those two, Rose and Mog, must have been meeting here summer after summer.

There were fewer people in the Club, and room on the floor for Chris to dance at his best – which, he knew, without vanity, wasn't too bad, given a good partner. Rose had taken off her sandals, and the idea of her being a sea-creature came to him again as she glided towards and away from him, following every movement, her dress floating or swirling, spiralling round her body as he span her round, and that body soft and warm against his, exciting him in their brief contact. Her look was intent yet faraway, all her mind given to the dance. But after a while her face changed: she looked past Chris, turned her head away as they twisted, and once or twice missed his signal, spoiled the movement. And Chris, whose eyes had been on her, and on the other dancers in their path, soon saw why. Nick was standing leaning against the door-jamb, watching them. The music stopped, and Chris guided Rose through the dancers towards him.

'Nick's my brother, Nick, this is Rose.'

'You came after all!' Chris was happy to see him, happy to have been seen dancing so well with Rose. Things were always better when Nick was there, and now he, Chris, had new friends to introduce. Nick on his own was not "family", but acted like a magnet on Chris, drawing him away from that ingrown life he was outgrowing. And here he had a breakaway of his own to show his brother.

It was no surprise to him when, as a new record was put on, while yet the needle could be heard scraping over the amplifier, Rose and Nick moved on to the floor. They danced together till Nick had to go with the man who had brought him. Chris felt no rancour. Nick's dancing was worth watching on its own, cool and sure, outstanding with such a partner as Rose.

The evening ended as no evening had ever ended for Chris – in a midnight voyage. After the heat indoors they were cooled by the easterly breeze, soon used to the darkness, lit by milky starlight that showed them the waiting boats. Chris, calling 'Goodnight!' to Rose and Rowan, found Mog and his small dinghy already afloat. There was room for him amidships with lightweight Tosh crouched in the bows.

Cries, laughter, the scrape of a keel, all noise grew fainter as Mog dipped his oars into the tide taking them upstream through the Narrows. Now there was only the sky, the woods slipping slowly past them, the stars. Chris was almost asleep when they grounded at the hard.

He waited while Mog made the painter fast on the pulley-hauley and walked over the fields with them both.

'Your brother,' Mog was asking, 'he's pretty smart, I should say?'

Tosh turned round: 'He's dishy. Dreamy.'

'What I thought.' Mog sounded disheartened. Chris was sorry. He liked Mog a lot. There was nothing wrong with the other cottagers; but Mog he might make friends with. He didn't suppose that Mog would be seeing as much of Rose as he had been used to, summer after summer.

CHAPTER THREE

Chris came down next morning to find his mother making breakfast.

'We've nearly run out of milk – could you go for it fairly soon? After you've eaten, of course.' She put out two milk-cans, well scalded.

It seemed to be settled that he should be the one to fetch the milk every morning.

Chris's first waking thought had been to go back to Garrow Cottage. And the farm was in the opposite direction, up-river. So he walked his fastest, feeling the contrary pull back towards Garrow. Trewin House stood high above the estuary, and as he climbed the stony track and crossed a granite stile into pastureland, more and more of the river lay before him. The morning was as yet still and grey; mist curled up from the water, and woods lining the banks seemed like herds of animals pressed together, creeping down from parched fields to drink, hanging their heads as they licked the salt water. Upstream the river, cut by creeks and inlets that could only be reached by boat, diverged, one arm stretching up to a faraway village, the other disappearing into mist. Trewin House was tall and narrow, lopsided, with a tower to one side sticking up like a forefinger, startlingly white against the landscape of small fields and granite walls.

A couple of horses lifted their heads as he passed, then returned to the hard work of getting grass from the dry pasture. Thistles there were in plenty. As the wind stirred, thistledown began to drift towards the river, and Chris understood what he had heard last night – how Mrs Trewin had let the farm to a farmer who, like her, cared more for hunting than farming, and how, in consequence of neglect, thistledown floated across to the other side, wide though the river was, and seeded the fields there.

Turning into a deep, lush lane that bordered Mrs Trewin's garden, he came to a gate. If he nipped through, he might save five minutes or more in getting to the farmyard. The garden was overgrown and as he pushed through bushes, tall eucalyptus and rotting undergrowth, he breathed again the spicy sub-tropical smell that had stirred his imagination last evening. He came out on a vegetable plot, and a man in a striped tee-shirt slashing at the undergrowth. His blue eyes were bloodshot, his hair gingery, his stylish duck's arse haircut darkened with sweat.

'I was taking a short cut,' Chris said apologetically. But there was no need to apologise.

The man nodded: 'Up the garden and across the drive – it's the farm you want?' He went on with his slashing, as though the rich wild growth was closing in on the vegetables and the most a man could do was to keep the jungle at bay. Higher up the garden was mostly grass, terraced with rock, rife with giant rhubarb and head-high ferns. Keeping to a path at one side that seemed to be a dried-up stream, making towards trees in the drive ahead, Chris heard a dog barking, and was confronted, as he stepped on to the gravel sweep, by a huge Chow with bristling fur and bared teeth. Dropping his milk bottles, he made for the nearest tree, an umbrella pine, leapt for the lowest branch and swung his feet clear of the dog, which barked and growled below.

A door opened at the side of the house and a voice cried, 'Bella, Bella!'

The woman who emerged wore a filmy garment covered with large crimson roses, and underneath, as Chris saw when she stood at the foot of the tree, a see-through nightdress, and gold sandals.

'What are you doing up there? This is private ground!' Her hand was buried in Bella's deep ruff, and Chris slithered down, mortified by his panic retreat.

He had come for the milk, he explained, had taken a short cut to the farm – the man working in the vegetable

25

garden had said he might.

'He had no business to!' Mrs Trewin, as Chris supposed she must be, glanced down the garden, speaking with such authoritative contempt that he concluded the man might be a gardener, though he didn't seem like one, liable to be dismissed out of hand.

'*I will have privacy!*' Her large prominent brown eyes stared over his head, and two spots of colour stood out against her creamy-pale skin. Her hair, high-piled in snaky coils, caught the sunlight filtering through branches. It looked, thought Chris, like copper – the copper ornaments his mother was so keen on, that she had lacquered so they would keep their shine.

She looked him over from head to toe, and he stood staring back, worse embarrassed than before.

'Come, boy,' she said, her manner changed, her voice light yet husky. Still holding Bella's collar, she turned and walked towards the house.

'Thanks, but I ought to get on.'

She seemed not to have heard him, and he didn't like to leave. He followed her down a dark passage and into a large room filled with light, with bare boards, scattered worn rugs, and not much furniture; but splendid views to the south and east. Eastwards the whole estuary was visible, widening past capes and bays to the mouth, and two headlands with the horizon drawn taut between them.

Most interestingly, a sizeable telescope was trained on that horizon.

The chow, let loose while his mistress made a clinking sound among bottles and glasses on a tray, sniffed round Chris, who remembered to put his hand out, palm downward.

'That's a funny name for a dog,' he remarked for something to say, as she turned towards him holding a small glass.

'Have some Madeira. Why? She *is* beautiful, don't you agree?'

Looking at the drink he began: 'Thanks, but I –'

'Drink up!' she commanded him, arching plucked eye-brows with a look which said as plain as if she'd spoken: Silly boy! It's time you grew up, and a small glass of Madeira so soon after breakfast is a small act of emancipation.

He sipped the sweet, warming liquid. Smoking continuously, lighting each cigarette from the previous stub, she sat on a gilt-edged sofa with the stuffing coming out, arranging one leg along the seat so that folds of rose-splashed nylon fell away. Chris still stood, not having been invited to sit down, though a suspicion, too awful to dwell on, suggested there was room for him at her foot, and that that was where he was meant to be.

'You don't answer. What are you thinking?'

'About Bella.' This was not untruthful, though he was thinking not of the dog but his own Bella at the fruit farm, realising for the first time that Bella meant beautiful, and at the same time that Mrs Trewin's leg was in marvellous shape considering how old she must be.

'I knew a girl called Bella,' he said. And at that moment, spoken of, as she was, in the past, "his" Bella floated away in his mind, insubstantial, evaporating in the heady distillations of the extraordinary life he seemed to have dropped into.

He looked away, fixing his gaze on the telescope, impersonal, dependable astride its three legs.

'Look through it if you like.'

He put an eye to the end that was towards him and began to move it about up and down and sideways, unable to focus on anything.

'This is my look-out post.' She had come up close behind him. 'Nothing happens on the river without my knowledge. No craft can pass the headland unnoticed. The river belongs to me.'

The proud tremor in her voice made him think: she's queer – mad, even.

27

'For centuries it has belonged to Trewins, the river. You may have wondered, boy – your name – I've forgotten it – did you tell me?' He told her, and she went on, 'You may have wondered at the dazzling whiteness of this house. Like a lighthouse. It has to be repainted every two years. For it is a landmark. Without it, no ship could navigate the river, pass through the rocks at the entrance. You are silent, boy. What are you thinking?'

'How is it you are called "Trewin" if you're married?'

'Married my cousin, of course. Let me look a moment . . . that boat out there.'

She raised the eyepiece to her own level and turned the brass focus-ring.

'Yes, as I thought, one of Danny Marsh's. She's quite unscrupulous. Lets dinghies out to duffers who've never rowed across a pond. I've watched this one all week.'

Chris's impression was that she would have welcomed disaster, eagerly awaited catastrophe.

'They're sailing better today. That fat fool isn't on board.' She concentrated: 'That young man there. From the holiday cottages, probably. But not one I know.' Her voice was a low purr. 'M-m. Like a young Greek. Ulysses tied to the mast.'

'Not tied to the mast, surely?' Chris already suspected the sailor's identity.

'No, no. Ignorant boy. I'll tell you about Ulysses some time.'

'I know about Ulysses. Can I have a look?'

She showed him how to focus and train the instrument, standing so close behind him that he smelled her body, a mixture of sweat and scent that was not offensive because the scent in some way merged with the sweat. He swept the telescope about; and with astonishing suddenness, so close and life-like that it was like running into them, there were Nick and Rose, he standing with an arm round the mast adjusting the sail, she at the tiller.

'That's Nick. My brother.'

28

'You must come again. And bring your brother.'

Her hands were on his shoulders, gently kneading them. Slightly sickened, he slid away.

'Thanks for the drink. I'm sorry but I must go. Mum'll be wondering – we've run out of milk.'

'That's not what you are thinking. Don't you ever say what you are thinking?'

He reddened. For what he was thinking was: that scent. Woodsmoke . . . kidneys for breakfast . . . horse-dung . . . Smells fascinated him, but this one eluded his experience.

When he was halfway to the door she called after him: 'You will come? Day after tomorrow. After supper. You can see the moon through the telescope – craters, canyons, mountain-ranges – and the stars.'

Her voice had changed as she spoke: the note of appeal, like a child left behind, made Chris sorry for her.

CHAPTER FOUR

Returning to the cottage with the milk, Chris found a note: 'Dad and I gone walking. Back for supper. Tinned pilchards in larder.'

Only stopping to fetch bathing trunks and a towel, Chris made off for Garrow Woods, climbing the steep meadow at a pace that made his back prickle with sweat. The sun was high now, and the day full of heat.

Once in the woods his pace slowed, partly because he had difficulty in striking the path and found himself knee-deep in brambles. But also because, when he stopped to get his bearings, the extreme stillness of the woods made him curiously wary. The stunted, moss-encrusted oaks crowded each other, only their interlaced branches keeping them from falling. Clumps of holly, straighter, more vigorous, further diverted his course. All, that summer morning, himself included, competed for air. A wood pigeon's cooing only emphasised the silence. Chris had intended to return to his viewpoint down the estuary, where Rose had found him. He would climb down the rocks and go in where the water was deep, yet clear enough to show wavering stones and weeds.

But the path – *a* path – when he found it, led him up, winding about and down and up again till he was sure he had missed the one he sought. Perhaps he was inattentive, and the more easily led by the woods, since his mind was so much on Mrs Trewin: sometimes she had seemed old, her face with its cracked make-up in the glare of the light-filled room, lines that narrowed her eyes, vertical lines that dragged at the corners of her scarlet lips – and, as he remembered now, a brownish channel from her nostrils to her short upper lip. Perhaps she took snuff?

And then again she had seemed quite young, as when he

had first seen her moving lightly and swiftly, great crimson roses billowing about her, from her door to the tree he had so shamefully shinned up; and when she stretched along the sofa, and those same roses settled about her body. He had never seen such a room, almost as big as the school gym. And the telescope – Nick and Rose. *That* set him off thinking on a new tack, till he was distracted by seeing ahead glimpses of an intense blue. Water – sea? Through the trees he could not be sure; but surely the blue was unlike any sea, even on picture postcards.

An upward turn of the path brought him out at the head of a narrow ravine filled with blue hydrangeas cascading down to a sunless inlet of dark green water. He stood where he was, needing to convince himself of what he saw, the intensity, the burning blue of the flowers. It was as though he had been brought there to witness what few people ever saw, for the path was hardly marked; and the idea of this profligate display, year after year, for no other eyes, perhaps, than his, gave him a mixed feeling: he wanted to keep it to himself; yet he wanted to share it. But with whom?

And as he plunged down the side of the ravine where the path led, Chris plunged also into a familiar state of longing and loneliness, a hole in the very centre of his being which needed to be filled. He slithered among layers of rotting leaves over black mud. Across the inlet the path continued, to be reached by balancing along a huge, fallen, slippery trunk.

But from the inlet's mouth he could see that he had somehow by-passed Garrow Cottage; he was nearly at the head of the creek. And it was the cottage he wanted, and Mrs Marsh and Rowan, not to be on his own.

He turned back and saw signs of a track following the shore-line. So much for the idea of the hydrangeas blooming for him alone!

The trees soon cleared; he recognised the path up to Garrow Cottage. But passed on, for there was Rowan's mother near the boathouse, scraping the hull of an upturned boat, whistling as she worked, a repetitive, tuneless whistle with a shake in it, like some un-English bird.

The black dog bestirred himself at Chris's approach, then dropped back to sleep.

'Hullo!' she greeted him without stopping, 'Rowan's gone into Porthmawgan for more paint.'

'Can I help?'

'You surely can.' She handed him a scraper. 'Never known so much weed. Don't reckon to cope with this during the season.'

Chris pulled off his shirt and began to work on the other side. The weed came off easily, but barnacles were stuck hard to the wood.

From time to time Mrs Marsh came out with some re-mark, a gentle grumbling sound half to herself, which didn't need an answer. At length she stopped, straightened, and came round to his side.

'Fast worker! You've practically finished. Go off, now, and have your swim.'

'I'd rather finish. I like work. I don't really like holidays,' he scraped away, 'not when nothing happens.'

'Plenty happens here. How did you get on last night?'

'It was all right. The best bit was going back afterwards by boat. It was a smashing night. They seem brighter and softer, the stars, I mean, and there are more of them than at home, at least you can see them better.' He paused. 'Mrs Trewin says we can go up and look at them through her telescope.' He felt his face grow hot, remembering her hands kneading his shoulders. And the way she called him boy, making him out younger than he was.

'You've been up to Trewin House?' She pulled a face, pursing her lips as Rowan had done during the Yacht Club dance, and Chris guessed she didn't much like Mrs Trewin. Hadn't Rowan said so?

Chris told her how he had taken a short cut to the farm-house, and how her dog had gone for him.

'I felt a proper Charlie up that tree,' he said, wishing he

hadn't let it all out. But she was so easy to talk to. 'Don't tell Rowan about it, please, Mrs Marsh.'

'Course not. And please call me Danny. Everyone does.' She was leaning against the boat, her arms folded. 'But there's no need to be ashamed. She's a bad-tempered bitch, and would probably have gone for you.'

'I can't make out how old she is, Mrs Trewin. Pretty old, I should think. But then there are times when she acts much younger.'

'About the same age as me – within a year or so.'

'Never!' In his surprise he looked straight at her with an expression which made her look pleased as well as amused. Her brown face was almost unlined and her dark, short, curly hair was hardly touched with grey.

'Perhaps I will go and have my swim now,' he said, looking away. He was unused to passing remarks about people's appearance, not older women; chatting up girls was different.

'You do that. Lunch'll be ready by the time you get back. You'll stay? We don't have much – cheese and fruit.'

'I'd like to.'

When he got back, having run all the way for the pleasure of it, the feel of the earth on his bare feet, and because he was hungry, Mrs Marsh had gone. He pulled his shirt over his head and went up to the cottage. Rowan had got a lift into Porthmawgan, which disappointed him. He had pictured her riding into town, throwing her pony's bridle over some hitching-post while she shopped.

He said as much when he was halfway through his plateful of cheese, brown bread and sweet pickle, in the cool, dimly-lit cottage.

Rowan looked amused, as her mother had done; how often he was beginning to notice a likeness between them. They had the same low chuckle: 'That'd be great! Only it'd take too long. And there aren't any hitching-posts left in Porthmawgan.'

'Can't imagine you except on a horse. Or in a boat.'

What Mrs Trewin had said wasn't true – that he didn't say what he was thinking about. Depended on who he was with.

'Rose isn't coming back, then?' Mrs Marsh poured black coffee. 'Top milk?'

'She's probably eating with the Travises. She went over after breakfast to see Mog. About the regatta.'

'She's . . .' Chris felt an unaccountable reluctance to tell them where Rose was – had been earlier on. But it was ridiculous. Why shouldn't he say? And they were sure to hear later.

'Rose is out with Nick in our – your – boat. In *Seamouse*.'

'I thought she'd be with Mog. The Porthmawgan Regatta's next week, isn't it? Those two have raced together for years.'

Rowan said nothing.

But later, when she and Chris were slapping dark red anti-fouling paint on the boat's hull, she said, 'Rose goes for older men. She gets hurt.'

'I thought all girls did – go for older men.'

'Yeah, well . . . perhaps. But not like Rose does. She gets serious.' She had tied her hair back in a red spotted handkerchief and wore a bikini which showed the hollows below her neck, and her small breasts. Her skin was an even brown all over. Except there would be paler bits underneath her bikini.

Sensing that her remark was aimed at Nick, Chris, for no obvious reason, felt a need to defend his brother.

'The thing about Nick,' he said, 'is that he's terrifically kind. Take this holiday, for instance. It was his idea. Because of Dad losing his job.'

'What does your father do?'

'He's a cabinet-maker. Been with the same firm ever since the war. They make antique reproductions – furniture. But they've been bought up – his boss died.'

'Won't he get another job?'

'At his age? He's fifty-six. Ten years older than Mum.'

34

As he spoke Chris worked steadily on, turning the big brush carefully from side to side so as not to splash the paint.

'So – this holiday?'

'Dicey, isn't it? Going on holiday just when you've lost your job. Mum and Dad took a lot of persuading – but that's what Nick's so good at.'

'I can imagine.'

Glancing across the hull, he caught the tail-end of a smile, amused, sceptical.

'It was me he had to persuade first. I was all set to go fruit-picking – I usually get some sort of job in the holidays. He said I must put it off, that we'd got to have a family holiday, which we haven't done the last three years – take Dad out of himself, back up Mum. And he'd pay half the rent. It was the advert gave him the idea. He only gets a fortnight's holiday, and he'd saved a bit to go off with his girl-friend, hitch-hiking across Europe.'

'Yeah,' she nodded, 'that *was* decent of him.'

He liked the thoughtful way she said 'yeah', deep and throaty.

She straightened up and came round his side.

'Fine. You've finished. So've I. Let's go and swim.'

As she padded along the path ahead of him, she looked back: 'But do they *like* sailing – your parents?'

'I'm not sure. They said they did, when Nick suggested the idea. Dad, specially, was keen. And Mum goes along with anything he wants to do. But since we got here . . .'

Nick was a great one for killing two or more birds with one stone. True, he had thought up this holiday for them all. But it was he who was keen on sailing. Furthermore, his girlfriend had stood him up. And his savings had somehow diminished, leaving just enough to pay for the boat.

There was no need to go into all this with Rowan.

They had reached the point and had climbed down on to slabs of hot rock before he continued, 'What they really like is walking.'

'That's O.K., then. There are marvellous walks – along

the cliffs as far as you want to go.'

She dived in; slipping off his jeans with his swimming trunks underneath, he followed. Afterwards, the rocks being too hot to lie on, they climbed up and lay in the shade of the trees.

A sail came into view, rounding the point opposite.

'It's *Seamouse*. They'll have to row – tide's running out fast.' As Rowan spoke, the sail was lowered and they came into view, Nick at the oars; Rose, steering, wore a floppy linen hat. 'There'll be no wind, the east wind dies out towards evening. They'll leave *Seamouse* on our mooring.'

Opposite, where the little point curved round protectively, there were mussel-gatherers. Chris recognised an elderly woman whom he had decided was the Travis's Granny. She had their fair colouring, and seemed twice as spry as Jack Travis himself, nipping in and out of boats, her jeans rolled up skinny legs.

'People from Oyster Cottages, aren't they?'

'Yeah. I suppose you know most of them by now?'

'I can't ever imagine getting to know them well. They're so . . .' Chris put his hands together with interlaced fingers, expressing his sense of their clannishness, a circle you wouldn't want to break into.

Rowan looked up sharply. 'They're not like that at all. Not stand-offish.'

'Not stand-offish. But they don't need anyone new. They all know each other and they're all related. And then,' he paused, 'I suppose this sounds silly. But why those funny names? Mog, for instance. And Tosh?'

'Mog's real name is Maurice. Who'd want to be lumbered with that? And Tosh – can't remember. Some name the little ones got wrong; and it stuck.' She regarded him severely: 'What a funny thing to mind. Don't your family have nick-names?'

'No. Anyhow, it's probably my fault. They're friendly enough. Suppose I just don't like people much,' he said with a touch of his former gloom. 'Not a lot at once, and all new. It's different with you and Mrs Marsh – Danny.'

'I suppose you think that's a funny name?'

'I don't.'

'She's called Dana. But she hates it. Let's get going.'

Nearing the cottage, they heard laughter. Mrs Marsh and Rose, seated at the garden table spread with tea-things, were laughing at Nick who was doing his cowboy act, wearing Rowan's hat. Chris wasn't embarrassed because Nick did it so well, recognizably John Wayne drawing on an imaginary adversary, tipping the hat over his eyes as he strolled across the lawn, bow-legged, tight-jeaned, turning the body over with a contemptuous foot.

'I was raised in cattle country,' Mrs Marsh said as Nick stretched out near her on the grass with a fresh cup of tea and a slice of cake, while Rose made room for Chris and Rowan on the bench. 'Those legs!' She chuckled. 'As though you spent all day in the saddle. Do you ride much?'

'I soon shall, down here. If I can get the loan of a horse.' He looked at Rowan, who didn't respond.

Chris surveyed the table, deciding where to begin. There was brown bread and honey, flapjacks and a squishy, mouth-watering upside-down apple cake.

'The Travises have a terrific boat,' said Nick. 'As well as the sailing dinghies. They all share this ocean-going – sloop is it?' He looked Rose's way.

'Cutter,' Rowan said.

'We sailed downriver and there she was, anchored inside – what's it called? Gwenan Bay. Sheltered by Gwenan Head, the big headland at the river mouth. She's black and white, gaff-rigged, with a tops'l. Looks quite old.'

'Old Mr Pernel designed her – that's Ben Pernel's father.'

'We went aboard. Whole crowd seemed to be there – a friendly lot when you sort out who's who. There was talk of a film. Mog, it seems, has ambitions to be a cameraman. A pirate film. *Werewitch* giving chase to a merchantman.'

'There's been talk of a film for years,' Rowan sounded bored.

'They're going to shoot it in a day or two,' Rose said, 'if the weather holds. And guess what – the ship that gets captured is going to be *The Elizabeth Jane!*'

Danny whistled. 'Clarry Trewin playing at pirates? What do you know!'

Rowan explained: 'Mrs Trewin doesn't mix much, not even with the natives. Let alone visitors, even people who've been coming here for years. She's a terrific helmsman, though. She and Jago between them – they'll take some overhauling. It should be good.'

Nick rolled over and sat up. 'You and I are booked to be pirates, Chris. And Rowan – blood-thirsty lady pirate with a knife between her teeth. Rose is to be one of the women and children on *The Elizabeth Jane*. Fate worse than death. Ravished. Horrid scenes. Very affecting. I shall be first aboard and make her my prize.'

'They can count me out,' Rowan began to clear the tea things. 'It's not my scene. Besides, there are the boats to see to.'

Twice during tea the phone had rung, boats being booked for the following day.

'That's a lousy excuse,' grumbled her mother.

'Not my scene either,' put in Chris, 'I'd rather help with the boats.'

'You'll miss a lot,' said Rose. 'The pirate ship's going to lie in wait off Gwenan Head –'

'Right out in the bay,' Rowan interrupted, 'tacking about in an easterly swell. Guaranteed to make you throw up.'

'That settles it.' Chris took the tray from her and carried it towards the cottage.

For the first time that he could remember, Chris wished Nick hadn't been there. Now, he supposed, he'd be around a lot. He had wanted to keep Garrow Cottage and the Marshes to himself.

As the two of them walked back to Oyster Cottages Nick said, 'You bloody turn out for the film. You're always sliding out from under, whenever there's a chance to meet people. Get to know them properly.'

'Bloody won't. I've met as many people as I want. Mrs Trewin, for instance. That reminds me – she's asked us to go up there tomorrow evening. No – day after tomorrow. She's got a telescope,' he grinned. 'Spotted you and Rose in *Seamouse*. You were standing up fixing the sail. That's why she wants us up at Trewin House. I should come. She's the queerest old bird.' He thought for a moment. 'She's not all that old. Only a year or two older than Danny, and she's about Mum's age, if that. It's her way of talking makes her seem old. She's got smashing legs.'

Nick, ahead of him, turned round. 'You *do* seem to have been meeting people. You make me curious. Perhaps I will come. If nothing else crops up.'

Nick believed in keeping his options open.

They emerged from the woods a new way, coming out where the cliffs were a good thirty feet high. A rope had been knotted round an oak tree bough, dangling to the shore.

'It must be super for kids,' Chris said, 'I bet Danny fixed it.'

'It's pretty super for us. Like an assault course,' Nick climbed up again, hauling the rope after him, and with a war cry swung down to the beach.

'They're back.'

The dinghies were on the pulley-hauley in Oyster Bay, small children were picking about on the exposed mud with buckets and oyster shells, and the rest lay about, some on the foreshore, others on the bank above.

'There's Mum and Dad,' Chris remarked. 'Wonder what sort of day they had?'

'And how they got back – we were meant to fetch them from the village. I clean forgot. I do wish Dad wouldn't wear socks with sandals.'

Their father, leaning against a tree-trunk, was offering his tobacco pouch to Jack Travis, propped up on an elbow. Their mother was talking to young Mrs Travis, who was feeding her baby, and the woman Chris had decided must be a grandmother had a toddler between her knees.

The Mitchells had had a marvellous walk, they planned to set off before the holiday was over and follow the cliff path as far as the Lizard. There was a Youth Hostel where they could stay the night if they couldn't get back.

As he listened, relieved that his parents seemed to be doing what they liked, Chris's eye was on a fair-sized sailing boat coming up on her mooring, just off the channel in Oyster Bay. Soon her crew, Mrs Trewin and the man Chris had seen working in the garden, rowed ashore.

'Who's that chap with Mrs Trewin?' Chris asked.

'Jago.'

He landed her where she could step on to the rough hard. The assured neatness of her movements and her clothes, a navy blue kilted skirt and a reefer jacket over her shoulders, made Chris look at her anew, with a respect that his mother's admiring comment put into words: 'Now, *she's* got style – Mrs Trewin, isn't it? Fancy going yachting dressed like that! It's apt to be muddy and messy, boating – she must be good at it.'

'Oh, she is,' agreed Mr Travis drily.

It seemed to Chris that her approach put some constraint on them all, lying around in their faded jeans, bare-backed, or in striped tee-shirts. Not talking much, drugged with the day's sun and salty wind out in Porthmawgan Bay. Mrs Trewin passed up the path with a nod here and there, followed by Jago with a string of mackerel.

Seeing Jack Travis, she paused. 'Well, Jack, we shall give you a run for your money.'

'If this wind holds,' he assented, sitting up with a reluctant, lazy grace surprising in a heavily-built man.

'It will.' Her peremptory nod towards the eastern sky reminded Chris of Mog's saying at the dance, "She thinks she *is* the river."

Her thick coppery hair, so wild and snaky this morning, was now coiled at the nape of her neck, showing the lobes of her ears studded with little green earrings. She might have been a different woman. Only her voice, the way she looked at people and things about her as though she owned them, these were the same.

'You're coming up to Trewin House, you and your brother. Tomorrow, wasn't it?'

'Day after. Thanks.'

'You'll all come – we'll have a party?'

CHAPTER FIVE

The next two days Chris spent mostly helping with the boats, swimming, or exploring the woods. He had begun to get used to the way Danny and Rowan accepted his coming and going. Accustomed, too, to their relaxed attitude towards anyone they liked. And towards each other.

The first afternoon, when Rose and Nick called in for tea after a day's sailing, Mog was with them. But the following day they came without him.

That night Mrs Mitchell said at supper, 'Why don't you ask Rowan back? You owe them hospitality. You might ask her mother as well.'

'I don't think they've got time. Danny – Mrs Marsh – works four nights a week at Porthmawgan Hospital. So Rowan has to be there for the boats, mornings anyhow. And then there's always the maintenance.' He was piling it on a bit, for there was no point in asking the Marshes over.

'Does she?' Mrs Mitchell took a professional interest. 'What does Mrs Marsh do?'

'Cooking.'

'As to hospitality,' his father remarked, 'I should think Nick's young girlfriend evens it up – supper, lunch – breakfast it was yesterday, wasn't it? Not that I'm averse to a nice girl around.'

'She came to breakfast because she brought *Seamouse* back.' Chris said quickly, seeing Nick's face perceptibly pale round the nostrils. He got like this when he was angry. Or hungry.

Nick pushed back his chair. 'Do me a favour, will you? Rose is *not* my girlfriend. She's teaching me a lot about sailing – she and Mog. They're a superb combination, know every yard of the river, where the currents are, how to – for Pete's sake, why am I bothering?'

He made to leave the room.

'Sounds like racing,' Chris commented, 'you're not thinking of entering Porthmawgan regatta by any chance?'

'Oh, very witty! Cut it out, can't you, and let's get this straight once and for all: Rose is a nice kid. And Mog.' This was an afterthought.

His father tactlessly pursued, 'My impression is she's fairly gone on you.'

As the door closed, Chris felt impelled to say, 'She's just a kid to Nick. He can't help it if girls go for him.'

Chris and Nick walked up to Trewin House after supper. No one else was coming. The party idea had fallen through.

Nick remarked, 'It's a pity Mum wouldn't have a go at the film.'

'How could she? She's much too old.'

'She's a darn sight more agile than some of those chaps – Jack Travis, for instance. She'd nip up the ratlines quick as I could. She'd have liked it so much – the whole thing.'

'Why won't she, then?'

'Dad, mostly. He's so much older than her, not just in years. So set in his ways. Living with him, she's got the idea – well, I s'pose it must make her feel old.'

'D'you think so? Maybe you're right. I never think about them much.' On reflection, Chris continued, 'She certainly runs around after him. He never does a hand's turn in the house. Perhaps he'd like it better if he was left alone more. I would. She runs us all around, come to that – well, not you. You're out of it, more or less. And look at this holiday – she fixes everything, same as usual. He sits about till she says it's time to go out.'

'He's depressed.'

'But Dad's like that all the time. Most of the time, anyway.'

'He can't help himself. With him it's a kind of illness. Everyone gets depressed. Look at you, lying about on your bed till Mum chivvies you out. It's your age. And you've got ways of getting over it, biking to Epsom and back before

43

breakfast, like you did once.'

'What about you?' Chris, unconvinced, felt accused.

'Oh, I could cut my throat easy, bad times.' Nick was evasive. 'With Dad now, it's different. As I said, it's like an illness. And he's got plenty to be depressed about.'

'He's always been a bit that way – if lazing around's what you call depression. That hut at the bottom of the garden. Down there for hours.'

'Wouldn't call that lazing. He's got a carpenter's bench and tools – makes things as well as mending them. Perhaps he should've done something different – designed furniture. If we'd had that kind of money. If he'd had the education.'

'Could be that's why he lost his job, being a bit on the slow side?'

'You mean he was for the chop anyway? The firm folded, don't forget. His age is against him – his getting another job. As it happens something might come up . . . but it's a hundred to one against. So I'm not saying anything.'

'He'll be at home all the time.'

'Basically, yes.'

Chris was silent, taking in the full significance of this. The holidays – his mother working all day. Just him and his Dad on their own. 'Sitting around.'

'Not necessarily. Just now, as I said, he's badly depressed. Being sacked knocks people for six, specially at his age. As time goes on he'll find things to do. Make things. Spend more time down at his work bench.'

'I'm thinking of the holidays.'

'You could do things with him. Go places, well, nothing that costs much. Walks. Long walks.'

'You wouldn't in my place.'

Nick thought. 'I think I should. For a bit anyway. It'd be worse having him on your mind, what he could be up to – or not.'

And perhaps, Chris conceded, Nick really might, for a short spell. 'I shall get holiday jobs,' he said. 'Call it opting out if you like, but I know I couldn't stick it.'

They had reached Mrs Trewin's garden gate, and Chris led the way.

At the top of the steep slope the tall house, brilliantly white, caught the westering sun. As they climbed up from terrace to terrace, Nick commented, 'This must have been a fantastic place. I suppose she hasn't the money to keep it up.'

'Money – it doesn't seem to matter much down here, not like in towns.'

'Money matters wherever you are, specially if you haven't got any.'

'It's easier to live without it though. Look at Jago – Rowan says he hasn't any.'

'What a way to live – being kept by Mrs Trewin! I bet he earns every penny, even if it's only for drinks and fags.'

'Paints.'

'Come again?'

'Paints, that's what he'd want money for. Rowan says he's an artist.'

They had reached level ground. Barking broke out in the house, and Jago opened the side door, holding Bella by her collar.

As they passed, Nick, fearless, bent down to tickle her under the chin.

'Shouldn't do that – she's a tricky old girl.'

The great room was filled with light, intense yet subdued, from the south windows. The sun had set, but the air was charged with this light; the river glinted gold, divided up-stream like a fork-tailed dragon.

Mrs Trewin moved towards them, wearing a long garment of heavy silk, striped blue, scarlet and gold, that hung from her shoulders to her gold-sandalled feet.

'I'm glad the party fell through. It's much nicer like this.' She looked up at Nick from under blue lids lowered over eyes that widened, stretched towards the outer corners. Like cat's eyes.

Nick walked away to the light-filled windows; the floor

45

was spacious enough for him to take several easy, bow-legged strides.

'She's got lovely lines,' he said. Far off, *The Elizabeth Jane* floated on the water, shaped like a small curled leaf. Or a quarter of orange rind, Chris thought, assailed, as Mrs Trewin passed him, by that same musky scent that had stirred his curiosity on their first meeting.

'She was designed by my brother. He was stationed in China.'

As she and Nick stood looking at the boat, Chris turned to the eastern window, to the telescope. Over the shoulder of Garrow Point the whole stretch of the river opened up seawards, pricked with lights on land and water. A half moon was already high in the sky, and he trained the telescope on it. It was true what Mrs Trewin had said. Markings could clearly be seen through the telescope which might be mountains and canyons. The surface could also have been that of a man's pitted cheek, marked like Jago's long face – as though it had once been peppered with cat pellets.

Jago was pouring out drinks. 'Our own make,' he said, bringing a cut-glass wineglass over to Chris. 'Parsnip wine. Two years old – quite strong.'

'It's like white wine.'

Jago fetched the jug over and refilled his glass. 'Come and have a fig. They're home-grown, too.'

The figs were hard, not so good as the Norfolk figs picked last year.

'I like that.' Chris was looking at an unusual sort of picture hanging on the wall, made of painted cement but inlaid with fragments of mirror that caught the dying light. 'It's a bit like the table you made for Danny and Rowan – made of the same stuff.'

Jago lit an oil lamp and held it up.

'It looks like an island.'

'It is. A Greek island.' Jago moved to another picture, holding the lamp close so that Chris could see how it was

46

made. There was glass in that one too, but most of the cement was painted in dark reds, blues and black.

'It's a woman. It's – is it Mrs Trewin?'

'You think it's like her?'

In a cruel way it was – a caricature of a woman seen in profile, but with two glittering glass eyes on the same side, two tears shining on the one cheek. And a black, plumed hat that made the creature ridiculous and pathetic.

Not wanting to answer, Chris turned away.

Mrs Trewin and Nick were sitting on the sofa, both smoking Nick's thin, black cigars. When she lifted her arms above her head the loose sleeves fell back, showing shadowy, foxy red fur in her armpits. So her hair was real, not dyed, Chris thought, disconcerted by the abandon of her gesture.

Nick got up and went to the telescope and she stood behind him, showing him how to focus the lens as she had shown Chris. But she did not touch Nick.

'The moon is too bright to see much of the stars,' she was saying, 'but if you turn towards the north you will see –'

'The Plough.'

'Everyone knows the Plough. No, look – just above the black curve of the hill. You can't see this star with the naked eye.' She went on talking in some detail, incomprehensible to Chris, who sat slumped on the sofa.

When Jago refilled his glass for the fifth time, Chris said, 'She knows a lot – she really knows about astronomy.'

'She does – she certainly does.' Chris detected in his voice the same dry tone in which Jack Travis had spoken of her.

'Why,' she had come over, 'the boy's half asleep. Are you sleepy, too?'

'Not me,' Nick stood stretching his arms against the dark window. 'This is my time of day – night, rather. About now is when I really come awake.'

'I think I'll go home.' Chris got up. 'But don't come if you want to stay. It's not awfully late, just that I'm so sleepy.'

'I'd quite like to stay – if that's all right?' Nick looked at Mrs Trewin.

'I'm a night bird too.' She smiled, and held out her hand to Chris. Her hand stroked his palm deliberately, as though she was wafting him away.

Jago saw him to the door. 'You'll be O.K.? Better go down by the lane. Easier at night. Want a torch?'

'Thanks, no. I like walking in the dark. And there's the moon.'

'Goodnight, then.'

Jago shut the door.

His way was easily seen. Only on the rocky path he stumbled once or twice. A little drunk, he stopped halfway down the lane for a pee.

A tree above his head moved its leaves like fish against the sky. A blue gum, Rowan had told him. The coolness after the hot room touched his skin, enfolded him. All his senses were stirred. He shivered slightly with pleasure.

Moving on, coming to a turn in the lane, he looked back at the lighted room. A shadow passed across one window. Long afterwards the memory of that room, which he was never to enter again, hung in his mind like a golden globe.

CHAPTER SIX

Chris did not hear Nick come in. In the morning he came to with more than usual difficulty.

'They're shooting the film today,' Chris reminded him.

When Rose came round, Nick was eating a late breakfast.

'You are coming, Chris?' She sat down at the table. 'Rowan's going to be on *Werewitch*. There aren't enough men for *The Elizabeth Jane*. You look enough like a seventeenth-century seaman just as you are.'

Chris, wearing one of the white, navy-blue striped tee-shirts that Nick had bought them both, supposed he might as well.

'What about you?' Rose turned to Mrs Mitchell, frying bacon.

'Yes, Mum – why don't you?' Nick tilted his chair and caught her round the waist. 'You'd look smashing being ravished.'

She would, too, Chris thought, seeing his mother in a new way, comparing her with Danny and Mrs Trewin.

'I wouldn't half mind – watch it, Nick – you'll have the pan over! Of course I couldn't.' She glanced at her husband. 'It's not our thing. Besides, it'll all be arranged, I expect.'

But she looked pleased at the suggestion.

'We can all – except Rose and Chris – go down to Gwenan Bay in *Seamouse*. From Gwenan Head you'll see everything. Ben Pernel's going to be up there with a camera on a tripod for long-range shots. Mog's on *Werewitch* with a hand-held camera.'

Rose and Chris, with the younger children from Oyster Cottages, were put aboard *The Elizabeth Jane* where Mrs Trewin and Jago were making ready to sail.

'Go below and get yourselves rigged up. Chris, you're

more or less all right as you are, with your jeans rolled up. That heavy belt's good.'

She herself was already dressed for the film in a green tight-fitting long dress with a very low neck-line, and a spotted neckerchief tied down over her hair. She was very much made up, but perhaps, Chris thought, you had to be.

Jago held out a red tasselled stocking-cap. 'Like some side-whiskers?' He was busy with a stick of greasepaint as he spoke. 'And a few lines to make you weatherbeaten. Roughen up your eyebrows – frown-marks – a proper old sea-dog! Ready?' he called back to Mrs Trewin at the helm, 'I'll cast off then.'

Mrs Trewin kicked the gear lever forward and *The Elizabeth Jane* slid through the Narrows, sails flapping in the head wind, as Rose reappeared with her flock of small charges wearing a pink candy-striped dress caught tight at the waist by a broad sash. Her fair hair streamed as the wind lifted and wrapped it about her head.

'No make-up for you, my love,' Jago said under his breath, just as the engine was shut off. The river was wide enough, now, for them to tack under sail alone.

'Boy! Pull in the starboard foresheet.'

Seeing Chris's helpless look, Jago hauled on the rope and made it fast round a cleat as Mrs Trewin swung the tiller over. The boat heeled, and Rose put an arm round the smallest children.

'Better take them below. They'll only be in the way. And for Heaven's sake tie your hair up!'

They moored off Trewin village, on the south bank, to pick up extra crew – three young children, a boy about Chris's age, and a man got up to look old with a long beard hooked round his ears.

From then on the day's events became increasingly confused so that Chris, afterwards, could only recall moments, scenes, as though he were spectator rather than actor. There was nothing for him to do, though Jago got him to pull on this or that rope: 'to look as though you're working the ship.'

As they neared the river mouth, breasting the incoming swell, the pirate ship was sighted creeping round the rocks at the foot of Gwenan Head. Her tops'l was up, the skull-and-crossbones flying from the masthead.

Instantly Mrs Trewin cried, 'Ready about!' and the chase was on.

Werewitch, with all her canvas set, was fast; but the smaller ship was more manoeuvrable as they beat, reached or flew before the wind. There was the added handicap of having to keep inside the river and the camera's range. More than once Chris was certain *The Elizabeth Jane* would crash on the rocks, heading at full speed for Gwenan cliffs and the roar of breaking surf; but at the last moment her skipper put the tiller hard over and they were set on a new course. Mrs Trewin looked splendid and intrepid and altogether admirable, and Chris hoped Ben Pernel, on the headland above, was getting some good shots. Better still, Mog might get some close-ups from *Werewitch* as they swept past at perilously close range.

Some of the "passengers" had come on deck, wringing their hands and crying to Heaven for mercy, the men shaking their fists as the pirate ship with its ferocious, raffish crew swished past them like a shark closing in for the kill.

At a prearranged signal *The Elizabeth Jane* allowed itself to be out-manoeuvred, caught in Gwenan Bay, and *Werewitch* closed with her.

'Fenders out!' shouted Jago, and Chris got ready to protect the paintwork as both ships came up into the wind, sails cracking like musketry fire; and the rattle of chain as anchors were paid out was the signal for Rose to reappear on deck with her only too realistically terrified band of small children, as the boarding party made ready to secure and board the hapless merchantman.

Nick, clinging to the ratlines, was the first to leap down to the deck. Rose detached herself from the children, ready to be ravished; but in the confusion something went wrong and it was Mrs Trewin who fell into Nick's arms, putting up a convincing show of resistance, kicking and screaming – yet clasping her arms tightly round his neck.

Chris, suddenly furious, tackled Nick in earnest, bringing the three of them to the deck. Mrs Trewin was thrown clear, but the two boys rolled over the cabin-top, falling into the scuppers. Nick, taken by surprise, gasped, 'Steady on!' Then, when Chris threatened to bang his head on the deck, he began more urgently to defend himself. Only the taffrail prevented their going overboard, and Jago, who pulled Chris off.

After that there was a gap in Chris's memory. He recalled being on *Werewitch*, his hands tied behind him, leaning against a bulwark, stiff and sore, and troubled in his mind. He had never fought Nick before, not since they were kids, and never so murderously.

The deck had been cleared for the final scene. The captives had been sent below. Mrs Trewin was privileged to sit in the stern and drink rum with the pirate captain, Jack Travis, disguised with huge black moustaches and a patch over one eye. At least she seemed unharmed (Chris turned his head to look and his neck hurt). Nick was there too, and other pirates, including Tosh, almost unrecognizable in her heavy make-up. Rowan, he noticed for the first time, was leaning over the bows, detached from what went on behind her.

'Ready!' shouted Mog through a megaphone, 'bring up the captives!'

Rose was the first to emerge, followed by a string of small, frightened, filthy kids, most of them crying, one with a nose-bleed running down his front.

'Terrific!' cried Mog, usually so amiable and considerate, his camera whirring, 'let 'em blub!'

A plank had been fixed over the starboard side and the "old man", after grovelling on the deck waving his beard to show how aged and infirm he was, was forced to walk the plank, which he did thoroughly, disappearing with a cry of despair and a splash. This made his children blub even more, uncomforted by Rose's assurances that he would come up the other side.

'That was great,' Mog said at last, coming over to Chris. 'It went well, didn't you think? The best bit was your fight.'

Afterwards Mrs Trewin and Jago sailed *The Elizabeth Jane* home, and the rest were ferried ashore for a bathe and a picnic. Nick sat with Rose and Mog and the others, as though nothing had happened. But Chris went off and sat on a rock, shaken, steeped in gloom. He hoped that Rowan might come after him – though it would not have been at all in character if she had – till he saw her in *Curlew* making for Garrow Creek.

The Mitchell family at length re-embarked on *Seamouse* and motored back through the Narrows, the parents full of the day's entertainment, not, it seemed, having taken in that Chris's onslaught had been genuine.

Not till they were alone, walking up to the cottage, did Nick ask, 'What was all that about?'

'It was Rose you were supposed to ravish.'

'Come again?'

'Don't you remember – at tea over at Garrow Cottage?'

'No. I don't.'

'Rose did.'

'Oh, balls. She didn't show any signs of minding afterwards. She put this plaster on my chin. How can you plan anything in a free-for-all in a film? You do what you're told. Taking direction, it's called.'

'Were you told to ravish Mrs Trewin?'

'Ouch!' Nick put his hand to the back of his head. 'For Pete's sake stop using that ridiculous word. It hurts to laugh. For a second or so I thought you meant to murder me.' He looked curiously at his brother.

'For a second or so I almost did. Can't think what came over me.'

'You must be sweet on the girl.'

'That's all you ever think about. As a matter of fact I'm

53

not.' Chris was thinking of Rowan. Rowan wasn't a girl you got "sweet" on. Rose, yes, Rose was. What he wanted from Rowan was something different, more complicated, quite what he hadn't yet discovered. Thinking of Rose as someone you could get sweet on seemed somehow disloyal to Rowan.

Crossing the road to the cottage, oven-like with trapped sunshine, he said, 'As a matter of fact I was beginning to think you might be.'

'I may be a lot of things,' Nick replied coldly, 'but not a baby-snatcher. I'm going in for a sleep. I shall probably be back late tonight.'

Chris followed Nick upstairs, still troubled by the unexplained violence of his attack.

'It was the way she went for you, Mrs Trewin. And you letting her.'

Nick, lying on his bed, blew rings of cigar smoke towards the low ceiling.

Chris went on, 'I can't make her out. She was absolutely super early on, the way she sailed, the way she looked. And then – to carry on like that, really going for you . . .'

'I can't say I minded.'

'No. You didn't. That was what was so . . . I mean, an old bag like –'

'That she is not.' Nick turned on his side and looked at Chris. 'She's more than super – and not just when she's sailing. Older women can be good value.'

'Why don't you go sailing on *The Elizabeth Jane,* if you're so stuck on her?'

'There are reasons . . . one thing, she's never asked me.'

And there's Rose, Chris thought.

'Furthermore,' Nick held his cigar butt between thumb and finger, 'I'm not exactly "stuck" on her, as you so crudely put it. She knows a lot. She's unique. But she likes things kept private, same as me.' He chucked the butt-end across Chris's bed and out of the window, and turned away.

54

CHAPTER SEVEN

Mr Mitchell sat outside the cottage gouging out a roughly hull-shaped block of driftwood. Two cans of beer, one empty, were beside him on the bench.

As Chris came out after breakfast, he said, nodding towards *The Elizabeth Jane* on her mooring, 'Going to try my hand at making a model yacht. Nick's taking us deep-sea fishing. Coming?'

'Not me!'

'You won't forget the milk?'

Later, making for Garrow woods, his reluctance to go for the milk every day hardened into resentment. Why should it be assumed that he'd always be the one? Nick would have gone willingly enough if he had been awake; but he wasn't to be depended on. This Chris accepted. But why couldn't their father go sometimes?

Chris thought of him sitting on the bench, with *The Elizabeth Jane* in mind and eye. It would be good, probably, when it was finished. Chris respected his craftsmanship. He'd sit there till their mother joined him, chores done, with a packet of sandwiches, rucksacks, whatever was needed. She'd even bring his walking boots out, and thick socks, the toes ready turned in for him to put on.

As he bestrode the wire that girdled the woodlands, Chris was surprised by a realisation: he didn't much like his Dad. He had this clear picture of him sitting outside the cottage, balding, his nose peeling, his hairy stomach showing between aertex shirt and long khaki shorts . . . but it wasn't his appearance. Chris's talk with Nick two nights ago had made him think about his parents as he never had done – almost the only discussion he and his brother had ever had about them. All this about "depression" didn't alter the fact that there wasn't much about him for anyone to like, let alone love. His being a bit pathetic only made things worse: who wanted to be sorry for their Dad? But surely you always loved your parents, unless they beat you or turned you out, like a boy he knew at school?

He took the path that went round by way of Garrow Point. How could his mother have stuck the life? Perhaps they weren't either of them very happy but stayed together the way most married couples did, at least where his family lived. He could think of people in their road who lived the most awful lives. But one's own parents . . . True, as he had said to Nick, he had never thought much about them.

His thoughts turned to love. And sex. The idea of the two of them together sickened him. Maybe the thought had had the same effect on Nick, who had told him, not long ago, that he didn't intend to marry. Well, not for ages. What was the point? The thing was to find a girl you fancied enough to live with – try it out.

He had reached the further side of the woods and stayed a minute or two to look down the estuary. Not far off, he spotted Mog's dinghy, white-painted, with a red sail. Rose was with him. A fitful cross-wind blew down a combe only to die on them at the next promontory. But anticipating how the wind would take them they were making best use of an inshore eddy, knowing exactly how close to shave the rocks and offset the slackening wind. As the boat picked up the next puff they were soon creaming along again. Chris had learnt quite a bit from listening to Rose and Mog and the rest.

The little boat was lovely to watch.

Further along the path he came on Rowan, examining a dinghy beached on the grass. She looked up and smiled, then frowned back at the boat. He came round to her side.

'Gosh! That's bad – how did they do it?'

About eighteen inches of the gunwale had been scraped and splintered.

'Oh – got rammed by a sailing dinghy and lost their heads, silly clots.'

'I think I could do a temporary repair. With the right sort of wood and some nails.'

'Could you?' She looked doubtful. 'She's got to be O.K. by tomorrow.'

They fetched wood and copper nails from the boatyard. Chris began to work on the boat while Rowan sat nearby, splicing a mainsheet.

Preoccupied by his discovery about his feeling, or lack of it, towards his parents, he needed time to sort things out. And it was good to have Rowan nearby, companionable in her silence.

As though he had been thinking aloud, he said without preamble, 'You seem to get on all right – more than all right. You and your Mum.'

Typically, Rowan's response was direct: 'Yeah, I suppose we do. We have rows of course. Don't most people?'

'We don't. At least, not Mum and Dad. Nick and I have the odd dust-up.'

'That must be pretty awful, their never having rows. Two people living together, they must get angry sometimes. If you can't show what you feel when you're angry, Mother says, it means you're too frightened to.'

'I wouldn't say they're *frightened* of each other.'

'Frightened of their own feelings. Look at kids. If their mother never goes for them when they're naughty they get scared: what they've done, they think, must be so wicked she can't do what they'd do in her place – go for them good and proper. It's the same thing for the mothers, she says – said once when she'd swiped at me. If they can't show what they feel, it's because they're afraid of how murderous they could be. I remember her saying that because it was the last time she ever hit me. About eight, I must have been. Just about too old for being swiped at.'

Chris was silent for a time. He had always taken pride in his parents' restraint towards each other. Now he saw it in a new light. His mother, it now seemed possible, took her frustration out on him. She was naturally strong-tempered and she'd show it, not by hitting him but by chivvying him, never letting him alone. She had been the same with Nick.

Chris remembered imploring her, not so long ago, 'Don't go on at him. He'll leave if you go on so,' and Nick had left. He remembered her reply: 'Someone has to. If I didn't "go on" at you both, as you call it, you'd never get anywhere. Look at you – all I'm saying is, you'll thank me for it one day.'

He asked Rowan, 'What do you have rows about?'

She thought. 'Small things, generally. She gets irritable, as you'd expect. Short of sleep. And I – well, I go dead quiet when I'm "in a state", as she calls it. That bugs her worse than anything, because I can't say what it's about.'

'You don't want to tell her?'

'Not that. We talk about most things. I mean I can't. Don't know myself. It's my age, she says.'

'They're always saying that.'

They talked of other things. Rowan asked him if he would like to help her set the mackerel nets she put out when conditions were right.

'You'd have to get up early, before dawn. It might be best if you stayed the night.'

By lunch-time the repair was completed and painted.

'Chris did a good job,' Rowan said at lunch, 'almost as good as they'd have done at the yard.'

Rose and Mog had turned up. Mog had to go off to Gwenan Bay. 'Coming, Rose?'

'I'd better stay. I want to wash my hair.'

When he had gone she asked Danny if they could have *Curlew* for the afternoon.

'We thought of going up to Otter Lodge, now your tenants have left.'

'Why not? It may need a spot of cleaning up.'

Rose said she would dry her hair on the boat. There seemed no question but that Chris would go too. On the few occasions when he had been alone with the two girls their tacit alliance had made him uneasy, never sure what they were thinking, whether they were secretly amused, would laugh together after he had gone.

Today, as they motored smoothly up one of the higher reaches of the river he had the feeling of being a captured prize animal – some sea-creature, netted like Rowan's mackerel.

Later he was to get used to these feminine cross-currents of communication, light and strong as spider threads, but this was his first experience of the kind, and he felt curiously excited as they turned in to the north bank where the boat fitted neatly into a small, rocky harbour.

As Rose, ahead of him, picked her way up the rocks, he noticed the gap between her shirt and her jeans. Certainly they were a very tight fit; Chris remembered Rowan's saying at the dance that Rose minded being fat. Curvacious, he would have said.

The path took them through a grove of young ashes and brought them out on a grassy space before Otter Lodge.

'There!' said Rose, as though she had some part in the place.

'It's really good,' Chris felt that praise was expected, and indeed, deserved. Otter Lodge was as good a place as he could have imagined, built of silvered weatherboarding roofed with wooden shingles.

Chris took a turn round the house. In a lean-to shed at the back he found a full can of petrol. 'Isn't this rather dangerous – so near all this wood?'

'I don't think so. We always keep some there in case people run out of fuel for their outboard.'

Rose unlocked the doors, opening up all of one side, and they stood looking westward over heather and rocks up the curving river. Here the woods were more open than at Garrow, allowing oaks and beeches to grow to their full stature.

Rose touched a young rowan tree near the house. 'Danny and Mr Marsh planted this when Rowan was born.'

Rowan came up: 'They've left everything tidy.' The

hearth was swept, logs stacked to one side, blankets folded on bunks and cooking things in their place. Only three mattresses were still on the floor.

'Most people sleep this way,' Rose said, stretching out on one. 'With the doors open it's as good as sleeping out of doors.'

Rowan filled the kettle from a can of fresh water and lit the Primus.

Chris sat down by Rose.

'It's *awful* being fifteen,' she said, 'neither one thing nor the other.'

'One *looks* so frightful,' Rowan joined them, lying on the third mattress. They all lay on their fronts, with Chris in the middle listening to the girls' desperate complaints. Rose's fatness, Rowan's thinness and her big ears: 'That's why I wear my hair like that – to hide the monstrosities.' And they both had spots. As for school, stretching timelessly ahead of them . . .

'The horror of it!' cried Rose, burying her face in her arms.

So tumultuous and confusing was the effect of lying between these two fabulous girls, who not only cared about his opinions but thought of him as someone who was likely, from his worldly experience, to have the answer to their problems that Chris, for a while, was speechless. Were they taking the mickey? A covert glance at Rowan's mouth detected no trace of its familiar ironical curl.

Yet their behaviour was not quite natural, as it would have been had he been alone with either. There was a hint of play-acting in their speech, as though they were imitating someone older than themselves, which had the effect of making them seem younger than they were. Surely they had not got him to Otter Lodge simply to complain about their spots? Whatever the reason, it was enough for Chris to be here, lying close between them; awkwardness, uncertainty, a pleasing tension were in the air, and his feeling was that his answers wouldn't much matter.

However, he began by assuring them that things would get better: 'By the time you're eighteen, say, you'll feel completely different.'

'We might be dead by then.'

Besides which, he continued, they had an unduly gloomy view of themselves.

'It's rot about your ears,' he told Rowan. 'People never know what they look like, they pick on something nobody else would notice. And everyone has spots when they're adolescent. Look at me.' He bent his head to show them the back of his neck, where a rich pimple was coming to a head.

'It's ready to be squeezed,' Rowan said, 'would you like me to squeeze it for you?'

'I will,' said Rose, 'I'm better at that sort of thing.' He underwent several delicious minutes of Rose's attentive fingers on a sensitive part of his neck.

Rose's fatness, when she returned to the subject, nearly stumped him. 'It's puppy fat anyhow,' he began.

'Then you do admit that I'm disgustingly fat?'

'I never said that. You'll lose weight, I expect. Or – anyhow it won't be all in the same place.'

'My bottom!' she cried.

'What there is will spread over more evenly – oh, I don't know . . .' He was out of his depth, thinking how she would need a smaller waist. 'I think you're super as you are – but if you wanted to be thinner I expect you could be. Anyhow, a lot of men like girls to be well-covered. Don't they?' He appealed to Rowan, who looked faintly bored, perhaps at having no defects left to complain about.

'How should I know? All I do know is it's much harder to put on weight than to lose it. And Rose eats all the wrong things.' She got up to fill the teapot.

'What I was going to say was, I think most men like two sorts of girl, one sort fairly slim, the other – well, like women mostly are in old pictures, with nothing on. They're usually fair, that kind. I'm pretty sure Nick does.'

'Does what?' Rose propped herself up on her elbows.

'Likes both sorts.'

'Hold on,' Rowan was over by the Primus, 'don't say any more about Nick till I come back. I want to hear.'

'What do you want me to tell you?'

'About his girlfriends,' Rose said quickly.

'I don't know much about them. He doesn't live at home, you know. And when he did he didn't bring them home.'

'I bet he tells you about them.' Rowan brought over three mugs and a tin of biscuits.

'He doesn't. Well, only in a general way.'

'I bet you talk about nothing else in bed.'

'You mean now – on holiday? I'm usually asleep when he comes in. And up before he wakes.'

'Comes in?' Rose sharply picked him up, 'where does he go.'

'*I* don't know. The eldest Pernel boy took him into Porthmawgan once or twice. Goes for walks. Sits on the beach with the others, same as me. You know that – you're often there yourself. Or he might go with Dad across to the pub in the village. They don't go much for pubs, the others in the cottages.'

Chris had not forgotten Mrs Trewin. But she was not someone to talk about, supposing – and there wasn't much evidence – she and Nick had got something going. 'I don't know why you're asking. What about you, anyway? He walked you home twice.'

'It was awfully early,' Rose said sadly, 'both times.'

'Nick's interesting,' Rowan said. 'I can't understand his working in a brewery. He doesn't seem that sort of person.'

'What sort of person *does* work in a brewery?' Rose spoke hotly, 'you're such a snob.'

'I should have thought he'd be at university.'

'He could have, almost certainly. He's the clever one in our family. It nearly finished Mum when he left at sixteen.'

'Why did he?'

'Wanted to earn money. He's keen on business. And I don't know what you mean about a brewery. This one's been run by the same family for a hundred and forty years. They make proper bitter, too. People come from all over London to get it.'

'Isn't he awfully bored working there?'

'No – why should he be bored? They're a nice crowd to work with. And not all the same. He has a friend there who went to Cambridge.'

'Boss's son?'

'Yes – so what? He has to work just as hard as the others – harder, in fact. Anyhow, as I say, Nick likes all sorts – gets on with people.'

'What else does he do?'

'Lots of things. Tennis. Pot-holing, sometimes, at weekends, but it's quite a way to get to.' Chris was warming to his favourite subject. 'He's quite surprising, the things he does, just what comes up, when he feels like it. He went up Snowdon once, wearing patent leather shoes.'

'What on earth did he do that for?'

'Because that was what he happened to be wearing at the time.'

The girls rolled over laughing.

'You don't seem to realise it was dangerous. You'd have to be fit to do it. Nick's always very fit. He was on the way back from Llandudno with two other fellows. They'd been to a wedding and a dance afterwards. One of them had a car.'

'Girlfriends as well?' from Rose.

'The girls were in Llandudno. Anyhow, Nick said he wanted to see the dawn from the top of Snowdon. He got the others to wait in a hotel.'

'And did he?'

'See the dawn? Not from the top. There was a terrific fog up there – it was light by then. And just when he was beginning to think he'd die without some breakfast a little train came puffing up from the other side – he was ever so surprised.'

'Had the others waited for him?'

'They'd have to, wouldn't they? They were asleep in the hotel lounge. After breakfast, Nick drove them all the way home to London.'

'That's *so* like Nick!' cried Rose admiringly. As though she knew him well.

The sun was shining down the river. A fish plopped.

When they had washed up the cups and locked up, Rose wanted to show Chris the tree-house that Rowan's parents had made for her. And, in a green hollow, the graves of six Lascar seamen who had died of yellow fever a hundred years ago.

'So far from home,' she said with her soft sadness.

Passing Otter Lodge again on their way to the boat, Rose stopped and touched the rowan tree. 'It's a good name for her, isn't it?'

Chris would never have seen this for himself, but now he saw the tree was like Rowan, with its slim, straight, bronzed trunk. Supple and whippy, Chris thought. Stand up to a gale. And its clear, deep red berries. Rowan red, her mouth was.

'Must we go back?' Rose said. 'Couldn't we sleep here? There's tinned food.'

'Of course we can't! We're expected back for supper. And this is one of Mother's nights at the hospital.'

'We do come up here sometimes and stay the night. It's my favourite place.'

'You're scared all the time,' said Rowan.

'Not all the time. Only sometimes, when I think of the seamen. Their yellow faces looking through the window. Not now, anyway. Only ages ago – when we were kids.'

'I like them,' Rowan said, 'I think they're friendly, the seamen.'

She went ahead. Rose lingered, still stroking the smooth bark.

'It's funny. This really is my favourite place. It's where I'd come to if anything awful were to happen – where I'd want to be. But I am a bit scared sometimes. Of the woods.'

64

'I should think anyone who didn't live here might be scared of the woods at night.'

'You think so? Yet I like walking in them at night. I often do, at Garrow.'

They had begun to trace the path to the boat. She turned round. 'There's times when I think there's a man following me. Even when I know there's no one for miles. I half want there to be, even though he'd be there to murder me. Do you think that's potty?'

Chris privately thought it might be.

'You know the lane down from the cottage? I once walked there slowly, on purpose. It was in the Christmas holidays, and there was frost and a moon. Shadows. He's waiting for me, I thought. Round the next bend, he'll be there.'

Rowan was by the boat, waiting to cast off: 'You steer, Rose. Or Chris, it's your turn.'

CHAPTER EIGHT

Chris returned to Oyster Cottages before his family got back from their fishing trip. Various cooking smells from the cottages whetted his appetite. In the larder he found cheese, ham and vegetables. He would make soup; he liked cooking. After a hunk of cheese and a can of beer, he set to. As he worked, he heard, not for the first time, sounds of altercation next door, confused to begin with, then with Jack Travis's voice above the general conflict. A child howled; was silenced; then it became a straight fight between husband and wife. Until his talk with Rowan, this was just the sort of scene that would have made him feel superior: his Mum and Dad would never have behaved in this way — and if they had done, not so publicly. The Travises hadn't even bothered to close their half-door.

The row died down, giving way to the loud general conversation which, with so large a family, was a feature of every meal. When he had got the soup on the Calor gas stove and cut himself another sandwich he went to the door and was surprised to see the Travis parents walking across the fields, arm in arm, with every sign of affection. Halfway to the beach they met his own family, Nick with the heavy outboard on his shoulder.

'What a day we had!' cried Mrs Mitchell when they were within hailing distance. She held up a string of mackerel and five dabs.

They had gone right out into the bay, and round Penmare Point; they had heard the famous groaning buoy, and seen waves breaking over the submerged rocks that had claimed so many wrecks. Nick had treated them to a pub lunch in a fishing village, and the reason they were so late was that they'd put in at the pub over in Trewin village on the way back.

As they stepped over the stile into the lane, Chris was pleased to see that they both had bare feet, as everyone else did, his mother's well-kept toes and rolled-up jeans followed by his father's less attractive feet below his unfashionably long shorts. They were definitely loosening up, the two of them, which was a relief – to see them slipping into the ways of the place, and presumably getting some enjoyment out of this strange holiday.

At supper all the talk was of the Porthmawgan regatta. A party were sailing round tomorrow on *Werewitch,* and the Travises had asked them to come along.

'You'll come too, Chris.'

'Not me.' His mother's insistent tone made Chris dig his toes in. 'There's plenty to do over at Garrow. I'd rather stay in the river.'

Working alongside Danny and Rowan, in and out of boats and water all day, salt-saturated, padding horny-soled along the woodland paths – Chris had so sunk himself in his amphibious existence that the idea of going into a town was like an animal having to change its habits. Furthermore he was reluctant to leave the safety of the river, to sail out into the open sea that stretched beyond Gwenan Head.

'Get some seasick stuff,' Nick suggested, 'borrow some from next door.'

'It's not just being *seasick.* I don't want to go.'

Mr Mitchell shifted uncomfortably: 'Better go, son. Miss a lot in life through not making an effort.'

Tension was building up, devious, subterranean, of which Chris's obduracy, his mother's will, were only outward expressions.

Quietly, with reproachful intensity, she said, 'You're *so* like your Dad.'

Chris stared at his plate, filleting his fried dab with extreme care. His father could be heard masticating; with his little finger he hooked out a small cast of bones and flesh.

Lightly, but deliberately, Nick broke the silence. 'Jack

Travis wants to teach Mum to steer *Werewitch*. Fancy yourself behind the wheel, Mum? You'd make a smashing skipper.'

'A piece of Mr Travis's cheek! That enormous boat?' She was noticeably blushing. Really pretty, Chris thought, taking a fresh look at her dark-feathered eyebrows and fine-boned cheek-line. Or could be.

'Big boats are easier to handle than dinghies. Slower to move, more time to think.'

'A wheel would be easier than a tiller,' their father took up this new topic, 'less muscular strain?'

Chris, still preoccupied with names, remarked, 'Isn't it funny how some people get called by their first names and others don't. Jack Travis, for instance. And Ben.'

'Comes naturally,' said Nick, provoking his mother to reply: 'Not with me it doesn't. I don't hold with all this first-name stuff. Not unless you know people well.'

Chris pursued, 'Whereas Mrs Travis – I don't even know her first name.'

'Delia,' Nick said. 'Young Mrs Travis. But Jack's Mum, everyone calls her –'

' "Mulley." It's a fish, isn't it?'

'Suits her. Always in and out of water, with a kid under each arm. In and out of boats. Always on the go.'

'She keeps herself fit,' his mother said, 'age doesn't count nowadays. And she hasn't an ounce of superfluous flesh.'

She got up and Nick stood behind her, slipping his arms round her waist. 'Talk about fit! You'll make a super Grandma, I can't wait.'

She detached herself. 'You a father? Need to learn some sense first – grow up!'

Her husband filled his pipe. 'Coming for a stroll down to the beach? There's that gallon of cider you fetched over from the pub, Nick.'

Chris had come to enjoy the odd evening with people from the cottages down on the beach, too good to waste indoors while the weather lasted. They would sit on after sunset in the cooling air, watching the afterglow reflected in the quiet water; even the youngest children stayed up. Being merged in a friendly crowd suited him.

But tonight he was the centre of attention, having to defend himself afresh.

'Not come to the Porthmawgan regatta?' Tosh looked at him as if he were out of his mind. 'But everyone does.'

'It's terrific.' Mog had finished applying a quick-drying topcoat to his boat. 'Not only the racing. But afterwards. In the inner harbour the dinghies have a fight – hundreds of us, sometimes. No holds barred – everyone trying to push everyone else overboard. We all end up in the water. Oh, and lots of other events. Dancing in the streets – pubs open till all hours.'

Had it not been for his mother's attitude, Chris might have given in. As it was he repeated sulkily, 'I'm sorry. It may sound crazy. I just don't want to.'

There were times when he cut himself off, even from people he liked, dug his toes in for no good reason. Did himself no end of harm, as his brother had pointed out. But he couldn't help himself.

As Nick went round with the cider jar, their mother could be heard from the bank above: 'I think everyone ought to make themselves do things – socially – even if they're not keen. My mother used to push me – I was ever so shy – and I've always been grateful to her.'

'I rather think,' Jack Travis's slow, resonant voice was audible through the general chatter, 'people shouldn't be made to do things they don't want to – social events that don't matter. Young people specially. There'll be such a lot they *have* to do – the really important stuff – whether they like it or not.'

Chris would have liked to be at Jack's school: he was headmaster of a big grammar school in the north.

A diversion cut across the discussion – the sound of horses' hooves drumming on turf. Rowan and Rose. They hitched their ponies to a post. Rowan's Stetson hat was tipped to the back of her head. Rose wore a velvet jockey cap.

'I borrowed Brownie from the farm,' Rose said, slipping down between Nick and Mog. 'We want to know about to-morrow. Rowan will be towing the dinghies as usual, in *Shearwater*. Mog and I – we'll be on *Shearwater*, obviously, as we've got to be there on time. And Tosh. We'll stop to pick up Binky over at Trewin Hard. He's crewing for her.' (Chris later identified him as the boy who had taken part in the film.)

Rose asked, 'Will you come with us, Nick?'

'I'm needed on *Werewitch*. Got to keep Mum on the straight and narrow.'

'You'll be better on *Werewitch*, too, Chris. Sure to be a swell.'

'He's not coming,' Tosh said, looking at him with curiosity.

'Not coming?' Rowan's tone of voice reminded Chris of Mrs Trewin. 'Whyever not?'

Nick craftily slipped her hat off her head, and retreated unnoticed into the field.

'I don't want to.' Had Chris known beforehand that Rowan was going too, he might have changed his mind. But not now.

Rose had been watching Nick; and cried suddenly, 'Not Snapdragon – take Brownie!'

But Nick had already unhitched Rowan's pony and was hopping about on one foot while trying to get the other into the nearside stirrup. After turning about trying to bite him, Snapdragon tossed his head and was away, as Nick flung his leg across the saddle and shortened the reins. Somehow his feet found both stirrups as Snapdragon cantered across the field.

'They're far too short,' Rose moaned, 'like a jockey!'

Snapdragon was now heading for the bank at the end of the field.

'Oh, God,' Rowan exclaimed, but not minding much,

70

'he'll jump it. As long as he comes off clear of the stirrups, and Snapdragon doesn't lame himself, get his foreleg caught in the reins . . .'

But Snapdragon stopped dead, shooting Nick on to his neck. Clearly enjoying himself, he wheeled, bucked and shot back the way he had come. Nick, unseated but not thrown, regained the saddle, the Stetson hat tipped over his eyes, his feet dangling below the stirrups, knees gripping, awkwardly tugging at a loose rein so that Snapdragon wheeled again, banging Nick's leg on the further bank, bucked, reared and made straight for the shore, scattering the laughing on-lookers.

Everyone but the Mitchells found the scene funny. Kicking up sand, Snapdragon splattered down to the water's edge, shook his head, trotted back and came to a halt near Mog's freshly painted boat, backed up to it and . . . 'Oh, *no!*' cried Mog. But oh yes . . . Snapdragon lifted his tail and let fly, neatly, into the stern, before Rowan could get to his head.

Nick's father was the first to move, scooping up the steaming dung with his hands. 'She'll be all right. Clean up easy.'

Chris walked slowly back to the cottages, hating the laughter.

Rose slipped her hand into his. 'He was awfully brave. He shouldn't have gone for Snapdragon; he'd have been all right on Brownie. But it was super the way he stuck on. He's got a natural seat.'

'He didn't use it much. It was in the air most of the time.'

'I mean, he could ride if he wanted to. Like sailing. He's a quick learner. Honestly, it was funny. But I bet everyone was impressed all the same.'

Seeing that Chris's shame was unassuaged, she went on, 'He did just what you said up at Otter Lodge. Nick always does what he wants to when he wants to, in his own way. It's terrific, to be like that. Not to mind what people say.'

'I should think he must be minding this quite a lot. Mog's boat and all.'

71

'He was brave and splendid. Don't forget to tell him I said so.'

Chris thought it unlikely that the incident would be mentioned by either of them.

He and Rose sat on the stone stile. From the woods an owl hooted, and was answered. 'That means the end of summer,' Rose said, 'the end of the holidays.'

After a while they returned to find the boat cleaned, drying out before it was repainted, and everyone settled again, Nick pouring cider, wearing Rowan's hat as though nothing had happened. In the meadow above, the ponies tore at tufts of grass, swishing their tails under a hawthorn tree.

Chris slid down the bank, avoiding Mog. Tosh came and sat beside him. Daylight was almost gone; but now the moon shone up the river, a great yellow disk rising over Garrow's shoulder, then free of the earth, growing paler and colder.

Nick offered his cigars all round, to keep the flies off. Mrs Travis took one. The older men lit pipes. The youngest children were drowsy or asleep, clustering round "Mulley". Mr Mitchell, leaning against his tree, held a sleeping child. Chris remembered from long ago the comfort of his Dad's soft tum, the smell of pipe-smoke, a kind of quiet bubbling in his chest.

Nick came and sat by Chris, and Rose soon followed. She leant against Nick's shoulder and he put his arm round her, with a friendly pat.

Later, when Rose and Rowan had cantered off, and lights were extinguished in the cottages, Chris, who had come up to bed, heard Nick's voice below.

'I do wish you wouldn't lock up every night. No one does here.'

In answer to some grumbling comment of his father's he said, out in the lane, 'Yes, I *am* staying up for a bit. Have a beer, take a stroll. Fancy sleeping on a night like this! All right, I'll lock up. If you must.'

CHAPTER NINE

Chris stood on Garrow Point watching *Werewitch* sail into view, take one long tack across the river mouth, go about, heel over, and then, with all canvas filled, sail out into Porthmawgan Bay for a long seaward haul before setting a course for Porthmawgan.

He had begun to regret his decision. Earlier, he had watched the motor-sailer *Shearwater* leave Oyster Bay towing a string of dinghies. Rose had come for Nick at an early hour.

'Nick!' she had cried from below their window, 'you're late. Everyone's waiting!'

Mrs Mitchell, from the kitchen, was heard saying, 'You'll never get him on his feet at this hour. Just you try.'

Rose took her literally, for her feet were on the stairs. Chris, beneath lowered lids, watched her curiously as she stood by Nick's bed. Would she tear the clothes off, rough him up, the way he did? Hardly. Nick's face was buried in his pillow. Tentatively she put out a hand, touched his neck, ran her fingers through his hair. He stirred, turned over and lay on his back, an arm flung over his forehead. For a full minute Rose stood there, oblivious, tracing with her eye the line of his nose, his full, half-open lower lip, his throat, his bare shoulders.

Mog's voice was heard in the passage below: 'Rose – Nick – put on your skates, for Pete's sake! Sorry, Mrs Mitchell, but time's short.'

Startled into awareness Rose vanished, Chris leapt up and stripped the bed-clothes off. Nick, half-awake, struggled into underpants and jeans left on the floor as he had stepped out of them, dived into a pullover and tumbled down the stairs, snatching a hunk of bread and marmalade held out by his mother in passing.

That had happened a good three hours ago. Now Chris, watching *Werewitch* disappear, supposed that Nick would have a kip on board. He had heard him come in: the square of window showed the half-light before dawn. Chris understood now that Mrs Trewin meant more to Nick than an "easy lay". Her strange ways fascinated him, her many-sidedness, her secret life. He would learn all he could in the short time left; and there would be an end of it.

Up till recently, his brother's love-life had been the occasion of curiosity, speculation and a degree of sexual stimulation for Chris. Not that he spoke about his girl-friends or brought them home. But in that suburban community, and with both boys at the same school, it was impossible for Nick to be as secretive as he would have liked.

Now that he was in digs, Chris only knew by signs when Nick was, as he thought of it, "on the prowl". It was true, as he had told Rowan and Rose, that Nick only spoke about sex and girlfriends in a general way, with a view to educating his young brother; his information was practical and to the point, though now that Chris, a slow starter, was beginning to date girls himself, he realised that his ideas about them differed from Nick's.

Having got to know Rowan he was more than ever sure that they did. As to Rose, she worried Chris; he saw what Rowan had meant when she said that Rose went for older men, and got serious. Standing by the bed this morning, he thought, she could have been any age. She loved Nick. This was not a word that Chris had heard him use; but it was what he believed he had seen on Rose's face.

His anxiety was selfish; of course he was sorry for Rose, uneasy about Nick's behaviour – more than that, he felt a vague sense of foreboding. But what worried him was how, if disaster overtook Nick's tricky two-timing – if Rose was to find out about Mrs Trewin – how this would affect his growing friendship with Rowan. It never occurred to Chris to share his anxiety with Nick, knowing as he did what his

74

reaction would be: incredulity. Rose was just a kid, a sweet, sometimes rather silly kid, and he, Nick, had given her a lot of fun. But nothing more. If pressed, he would admit: well, yes, she seemed to want affection, a bit of a waif, you could say. Chris could hear his tone of voice.

He would quite like to talk to Danny about it.

Approaching the boathouse, he heard the telephone extension ring and sprinted to get there before Danny, presumably asleep up at the cottage, heard it. Someone wanted a motorboat for a fishing expedition tomorrow. He consulted the duplicate calendar that Rowan kept up to date. The bell rang several times: he liked the feeling of being in charge. He checked a couple of engines, cleaned some plugs, and tried his hand at splicing a halyard. There was not really much work to be done, apart from the job of being there – at Oyster Cottages he had exaggerated the work to explain his days spent over here, at the same time dreading that, if he was too specific, for instance over the repair job he had done on the dinghy's gunwale, his Dad might suggest coming over himself. It was so exactly what he would have enjoyed.

His parents had come over once to tea, and Danny had returned their visit, the day he and the girls had gone up to Otter Lodge. Politeness was satisfied.

He looked for work to do, busying himself unnecessarily to fight a growing irritation that soon amounted to near-despair: his mind was on the regatta, all that he might be missing. And for why? That was what bugged him. The answer was only too plain. His mother's: "Cutting off your nose to spite your face" summed it up. It wasn't so much what he might be missing as that, once again, as Nick was always nagging him about, he had "opted out". And Rowan had gone. He had been so sure she wouldn't – for no good reason.

Having got a family party off in *Curlew*, it occurred to him that Danny was probably awake. He might even go up to the cottage and get lunch ready for her. At the foot of the path up to the cottage he heard what was strange at this time of year – the whine of a chain-saw. Following the sound along the river path to the hydrangea ravine, he came on Danny herself, and was in time to see a tree fall near the mouth of the inlet.

She turned off the petrol engine and grinned happily: 'Isn't it terrific? It's just come.'

'Isn't it too heavy for you?'

'Not a bit. Up to now I've had to use an axe, or get in Steve from the boatyard to help with a crosscut saw. Wait till next winter! I aim to clear the woods – that tree's rotten or of course I wouldn't have felled it now. I wanted to try the saw out.'

'It'll take you years – clearing the woods.'

'Maybe; but I can do a bit at a time, so much every winter. If the scrub oaks were felled beech trees would grow naturally, as they do up near Otter Lodge, gradually take over, and let in space and light. I shall make a clearing down from the lane, put down hard-core, so that people can drive their cars down to the boathouse instead of leaving them behind the cottage and coming through our garden.'

'That'll take you years, too?'

They had begun to walk back, Chris shouldering the chain-saw which proved as heavy as he had guessed.

'Not years. With a bit of help I can get it done by next spring. We'll leave the saw in the boathouse.' She bent to examine the halyard of a beached dinghy. 'That end needed whipping – did you do it?'

'Yes. I thought you'd be asleep. I answered the phone twice and sent some people out in *Curlew*.' He unhooked the clipboard for her inspection.

'That was decent of you. I got up early, when the chain-saw was delivered, thought damn the boats! For once I'd take the morning off and try it out. And you were here all the time. Let's go up to lunch.'

Tucking into home-made wholemeal bread, three sorts of cheese, and fresh pineapple, he thought what an interesting person she was with her delight in chain-saws and boat machinery, yet eating at a dark polished table set with delicate china, a fruit dish like a cabbage leaf, and small curved silver butter knives.

Over coffee, she asked, 'Why didn't you go with the others to the regatta?' She looked amused and curious, not in a nosy way, but with a genuine interest that encouraged people to tell her things.

'No special reason. I just didn't want to.'

'I thought you might have quarrelled with Rowan. She's pretty sharp sometimes.'

'About Rose, you mean?'

'I hadn't anything special in mind. Only that Rowan can be off-putting when she's in a cranky mood.'

'She's not off-putting. At least not with me.' He remembered that first night at the dance and Rowan's polite way of disengaging herself from people she didn't want to talk to.

He pushed back his chair. 'I wish now I had gone.' He walked over and leant against the door-jamb. 'It was something Mum said – the way she said it. She doesn't realise – thinks of us as kids, even Nick, though less so now he's got out.'

The silence, the emptiness of the garden and the surrounding woods were unbearably oppressive. He had been on the point of delivering himself of an incoherent jumble about family life, about Nick and Rose and Mrs Trewin.

He turned back into the room, put his hands up on one of the low beams and swung his body forward like a man crucified. Everything seemed pointless, his mind a blank, his family irrelevant.

'What the hell . . . Thanks for the lunch, Danny.'

He swung back on his heels and began to run, over the threshold, across the garden and through the woods. Boredom, emptiness, frustration added up to intolerable pain. He jumped the fence and ran all the way down to Oyster Cottages.

Here he scrambled for his sneakers under the bed, thud-ded down the wooden spiral stairs, out into the hot lane and up to the track that led across the moor to the main road, only slowing down when his heel began to hurt. Hop-ping, he removed the shoe, shook out a stone, and settled down to jog-trot.

He was going to get to that bloody place, Porthmawgan, if he had to run all the way. Seven miles? Once on the road he could pick up a hitch, surely.

On top of the bare moor the heat suited his mood. About halfway across he slowed to a walk; he began to limp. Sweat poured down over his eyes. He hardly noticed the scrunch of tyres behind him, but the old-fashioned hooter pulled him up, and he stepped to one side.

The bonnet of a Rolls-Royce slid by, stopped.

'You all right?'

It was Jago. Sitting beside him, Mrs Trewin, wearing a wide-brimmed straw hat, leaned forward: 'Get in!'

Jago felt for the polished brass handle of the rear door and Chris got in. The Rolls moved on as smoothly as the rutted track would allow, while Chris leaned back against the buttoned upholstery. In no time they reached the gate that shut the moor off from the road. Without turning her head, Mrs Trewin said: 'Open the gate, will you?'

Chris did so, and waited to close it. The car door swung open again and he sat back, while they moved off, this time with perfect smoothness on the macadamized surface. Mrs Trewin turned slightly: 'Your foot, boy. You've in-jured it?'

'A blister, I think. I've got used to not wearing sneakers.'

'Show me.'

'I couldn't, really. I'm afraid my feet are pretty filthy.'

Jago slowed down, but Mrs Trewin laid a hand on his arm.

'We can't stop—we're late as it is. Come on, boy, take your shoe off.'

Taking care to avoid touching her flowered chiffon dress,

Chris stuck his foot between her and Jago.

'Mm, yes.'

In some awful way, Chris felt, she enjoyed holding his foot, and running her hand up his leg. She wore a large cold emerald ring.

'A blister, as you say. We must hope it doesn't burst till you get back to the river. Filthy indeed – blood-poisoning. Try not to walk on it till you can plunge it into salt water.'

Chris withdrew his foot.

Mrs Trewin twisted round to look at him; her hat fell off. 'Sea-water is the Great Healer. Once back by the river you can keep your foot under till nightfall. Jago shall take you back, after dropping me at Lady MacCallum's. No other medicaments, remember.' Her soothing, sing-song voice nevertheless rang with insistence. 'Our bodies are nine-tenths sea-water. Did you know that? We are sea creatures by nature. From the sea we came, and to the sea we shall return.'

Chris had recovered sufficiently to notice that the "main road" was no more than a twisting lane: they had met no other vehicle, nor could anyone have passed them. The idea that he could have hitched a lift he now saw for the madness it was. He rested his head on the cushions. The smell of old, worn leather was curious and not disagreeable; perhaps it was that and the heat which made him sleepy, incurious as to where he was being taken. They turned in between stone pillars and came to a halt, after a twisting drive between banks of those same blazing blue hydrangeas, in the forecourt of an old, low stone house.

Jago reached across Mrs Trewin and opened her door, picking up her hat before she could tread on it.

As they drove away the breeze fluttered about her long dress, lifting fin-like wisps of chiffon. She held her large hat in both hands waiting for the front door to be opened. Chris felt sad for her; and a reluctant admiration. Something about the cut of her straight back reminded him of Rowan.

Once through the gates, Jago stopped. 'Where were you making for?'

'Porthmawgan, actually.'

'You'll be lucky!'

'I *was* lucky, being picked up. I don't want to go back. If you wouldn't mind dropping me somewhere? I was thinking of hitching a lift – rather more of a main road. If you could?'

'Like to hop in front?'

'She's super, isn't she?' Chris said as they coursed along, '1924?'

'Yes. She's a beauty.'

'Is it true you never have to do anything to the engine?'

'Never. I couldn't if I had to. She's serviced twice a year. Not that she gets out much, poor old girl.' He patted the door panel through the open window. 'Where was your rendez-vous?'

'Pardon?'

'Where are you supposed to meet your friends?'

'They don't know I'm coming. But I can't miss picking out the boat – *Werewitch*.'

'You don't know Porthmawgan in regatta week!'

'I don't know it at all.'

'Tell you what I'll do. Run you out to Porthmawgan Castle. The big boats come in last – their race ends late, as they go way out to sea. You'll be in time to see the finish, with any luck. And keep a look out for where they fetch up.'

'That's terribly decent of you.'

Jago looked amused. 'You're picking up the lingo, as Nick would say.'

Chris did not pretend to understand what he meant.

They were descending a winding hill. All about them, and below, the town was spread out. Beyond lay a great stretch of water, Porthmawgan Roads, bounded on the far side by a long peninsula. There were cranes, large coasters, an oil-tanker, harboured from the open sea. Upstream, houses reached further than he could see.

'But it's enormous!'

'Sizeable. How's Rowan?'

'She's all right,' Chris replied awkwardly, embarrassed, but not displeased to be coupled with her.

Jago, looking ahead, went on, 'She's an extraordinary girl. But then so's her mother. They belong to the place. Or rather, Danny's made it theirs. Made it for Rowan – a place to be.'

'A place to be. From the first day, I felt that.' Jago, it seemed, might understand – had put into words the essence of what Rowan and her mother meant to him.

'Most people haven't got it nowadays. And it's getting worse. That's why I dropped out – left London.' Jago ran a hand through his straight, greasy, dark red hair, a gesture of weariness. 'Not that it worked out – not for me.'

They halted at traffic lights. When the lights changed, the Rolls, like an elderly expert skater, wheeled right, glided from gear to gear till they were skirting the town, the blue bay spread out before them, the horizon softened by a premature autumnal haze.

Jago continued: 'They certainly picked me up, Rowan and Danny.'

'I don't understand quite – can't make out the way Danny lives. She has everything so . . . so nice.' (His mother's unspeakable word "dainty" had checked him.) 'In the house. Yet to see her outside, she could be a sort of lumberjack, a boatman, liking engines and so on. And her chain-saw – she's just bought that.'

'I don't think she likes it all that much. It's what she had to learn to do, if they wanted to go on living there. She needs a man about the place.'

'She gets Steve down from the boatyard if anything's too heavy for her.'

'That wasn't what I meant. She must have been the most beautiful girl imaginable – a real knockover, when she came over from the States. Still is, for my money.' Jago changed gear, noiselessly, and continued, 'So Danny's bought a chain-saw?'

'She can use it, too. Says she's going to make a road down to the boathouse.'

Jago threw back his head and snorted: 'Poor old Clarry!'

'Why?'

'She blows her top every time Danny fells a tree. Danny does it partly to annoy. Clarry hates her.'

'You'd think she'd like to have the place kept nice.'

'You don't know Clarry.'

'I think I do.' Chris was remembering the talk that first night at the club dance. 'Does she think of herself as – as a sort of priestess, and the woods as a sort of sacred place?'

Jago had brought the Rolls to a halt. 'You're – what's the word? – percipient. That's just about what she does think.'

'Why does Mrs Trewin hate Danny? I don't see how anyone could.'

'Several reasons. Mostly because Rowan stands to inherit Garrow after her death. It's no use, of course, financially. They'll never keep it up. And they're not allowed to build on it. I suppose the National Trust may take it over.'

'Rowan – she'll own the woods, the foreshore, the cottage? How . . . no, don't tell me, more cousins?'

'Something of the sort.'

Silence fell while Chris took in this new view of Rowan as a woman of property.

He had been longing to say, 'Why don't you go back and help Danny?' But at the mention of Mrs Trewin a closed look had come over Jago's sallow, long-jawed face. Nick, too, could put on that shuttered, keep-off expression.

Jago leant over him and opened the door: 'You'll be all right now? Follow the signpost. Hope you see *Werewitch* come in and meet up with Rowan and the rest.'

The engine was still idling and Chris couldn't resist holding his watch to his ear: 'Is it true what they say, that you can hear your watch ticking over the sound of a Rolls engine?'

'That wouldn't be too difficult. No – it's said to be the clock on the dashboard. Ours stopped ages ago.'

With a word of thanks Chris got out and shut the door, carefully not slamming it.

Jago and the Rolls, reversing gracefully, purred back up the hill.

CHAPTER TEN

Following the signpost saying "Porthmawgan Castle" Chris found his way among council house gardens, ablaze with dahlias and michaelmas daisies, a factory and a school, to a worn track along a promontory with the castle, fortress-like, at the end, marking the river mouth. People were coming and going, the redoubt was crowded, and he took time finding a point of vantage. Leaning over the parapet he saw the yachts, their great sails filled, racing for home, hardly close enough, yet, for identification.

A man next to him, lifting field-glasses, cried: '*Oregon II* is in the lead. Another of those modern racing hulls lying second – *Starquest*, I think. Then *Werewitch*, fine old war-horse, lovely to look at but no match for these new ocean-going streamlined jobs.'

His friend, on Chris's right, rejoined, 'Ocean-going my foot! *Werewitch's* been round the world – 1937, wasn't it? Well, not far off it. Far East. I remember, having just joined the R.N.V.R. myself. Young Marsh – R.N. of course – was posted to the China Station, where his uncle was. Whole family turned out, sailed his young wife round by sea. Typical. Mad as hatters, the lot. But unbeatable. I'll lay you a fiver *Werewitch* comes in first. Always does.'

'Done!'

Chris, distracted by the talk, now recognized *Werewitch*, making no frantic attempt that he could see to overtake the two yachts ahead of her which were on a tack that would keep them well clear of a small island, hardly more than a rock, marking the end of a partially submerged reef that ran out from the opposite shore. All sails set, *Werewitch* altered course as she approached the island, and the entrance to the river.

The man on his right chortled, 'Oho, so that's what

they're about – taking a chance – sailing *inside* the island! Terrific risk, but it'll put them ahead of the other two.'

'Never! They'd hit the rocks, even at the top of the tide. By God – you're right! You say they're a crazy lot. Must be. Suppose the wind dies. At best they'll have to put on the engine and be disqualified.'

'*Werewitch* hasn't got an engine.'

The two men, with Chris between them, watched the cutter shoot through the gap, take the wind out of *Oregon's* sails as she passed across her bow, making for the castle shore and the final tack that would bring them into Porthmawgan Roads.

It was on this tack that their tops'l began to shiver.

'There's something wrong . . .' The man had no time to finish as the boat heeled sharply over, and in that split-second a man ran up the mainsail, freed a halyard and slid down a shroud as the tops'l filled and *Werewitch* sailed past the castle. On the ramparts above, a gun boomed. *Werewitch* had won!

Chris found himself jumping up and down, shouting incoherently, not yet fully realising the unique daring of the feat he had just witnessed.

The man on his left shouted, 'Wouldn't have believed it if I hadn't seen it! Who was the chap?'

'Ben,' shouted Chris, 'Ben Pernel!'

The man on his right who had known Rowan's father dabbed at the corner of his eye. 'This damned wind! Come on, let's go.'

Chris left them and began to run, forgetting his blister, making for the town, the docks, the harbour. He had passed the council houses before, slowing to a walk, he remembered that he hadn't stayed to watch where, in all that great stretch of water, *Werewitch* had sailed to. He didn't worry unduly. Someone would be sure to know.

Nearly two hours later he limped into the narrow streets of the town.

The crowds were unbelievable, jam-packed from pavement to pavement, between illuminated shop-fronts, under coloured lights. In these narrow streets it seemed later and darker than it was. He attempted to squeeze his way more or less in the direction of where he supposed the waterfront to be. Happy, drunk, indiscriminately affectionate or amorous, arms intertwined, the revellers carried him this way and that till he lost what little sense of direction he had had. The side streets were no better.

Smells of frying filled the stagnant air. Chris realised simultaneously that he was dying of hunger; and that he had no money on him.

In extremis, summoning his last reserves of strength, he forced his way down a narrow cobbled lane ending in a flight of steps, and found himself where he needed to be, on the waterfront. Though darkness had not yet fallen, arc lights were already reflected in the oily water, cranes black against the deepening blue sky.

Here there were few people; the breeze was reviving. He found a man who looked like a seaman.

'Regatta? You want the inner harbour, that's where the fun is.'

'No, no. At least I don't think so. I must find *Werewitch* before she sails.'

'One o' they big yachts? There be one now, catching the tide.'

There, unmistakably, was *Werewitch*, ghosting half a mile away towards the open sea.

Chris sat down on a bollard.

He supposed he could doss down somewhere. For the first time since coming to Cornwall, he felt cold as well as empty. Doss down, hitch a lift in the morning. No way of letting anyone know. He'd ring Rowan up first thing – borrow twopence for a callbox. He even remembered the hospital – Danny might be there! But it was one of her nights off. One thing was certain, he wasn't going to ring them now, have Danny driving out. He'd asked for it, and he'd bought it.

He dismissed the possibility that *Shearwater* might still be somewhere around. Those dinghies that Mog had talked about, having jolly fights. But that must all be over hours ago. After a rest, he decided to get a little way out of town, find a haystack or a barn. Porthmawgan was built on steep hills, terraced, one street joined to another by steep flights of steps.

After two such flights, and the pushing and the tumbling in between, he sat down, halfway up the third.

Here a miracle occurred, or so it seemed to him in his collapsed state.

Up the steps came Rowan, Mog, Rose and Nick.

'Chris!' Rowan said severely (not unlike her Trewin cousin). 'What on earth are you doing?'

'I decided to come after all.'

'For Chrissake! You need a drink,' Nick squatted beside him.

'Food's what I need.'

'Hold on a sec – I'm just going up to The Swan to change a cheque.'

The others sat down on the steps, one above the other, to keep clear of the drunks.

'What does he mean, "change a cheque"?' Rowan asked, still severe.

'Cash one, of course.'

Mog remarked, 'I thought a pub was the one place they would never cash cheques.'

'Nick can sometimes. It's being in the trade, I suppose.'

Rose said, 'He's got a friend at The Swan. That's the only reason we're here. I'm jolly glad we are.' She looked at Chris with concern.

Nick brought down a tray of cider, crisps, and two pints of bitter for Chris and himself.

They had already eaten. But later they sat in a café and watched Chris stuff himself.

Watching the chips go down, Nick unobtrusively shelled out a seasick pill and made sure Chris swallowed it. 'It'll have more time to work. *Shearwater* rolls quite a bit.'

Rose was holding a silver cup.

'You and Mog won your race then? Congrats.'

'They always do,' Rowan spoke more warmly, seeing that Chris was restored.

They had met the crew of *Werewitch* and heard how she had outwitted her rivals. But Chris's account, seen from the castle, added dramatic force to the story of Ben Pernel's marvellous feat when freeing the topsail.

'He simply *levitated* up the mainsail – one moment the boat was sharply heeled over – the next she was back on an even keel, and old Ben sliding down a – a shroud, would it be? – and *Werewitch* dead on course for the finish.'

He sat with his foot up, enjoying the sense of involvement, of having after all made the regatta, and to some purpose. Rose, who had found an all-night chemist, put a pad on his blister, which was broken, raw and dirty.

Making their way back to the inner harbour they avoided the crowds by keeping to an upper lane. The fiesta was still in full swing, with the sound of rock echoing across the water, lights festooned along the front, and dancing on the cobbles in front of the old, colour-washed houses.

Tosh was there, dancing with the boy who had crewed for her. Mog looked hesitantly at Rose, then sat down by Chris as she took Nick's hand and joined the dancers.

'Come on,' Rowan invited Mog.

But in less than five minutes they came back to Chris. 'I've just seen a chap I want a word with,' was Mog's excuse. 'D'you mind Rowan? He'll be leaving any time.'

Left with Chris, Rowan pursed her lips as her mother did, indicating disapproval. But she said nothing except, 'Does your foot hurt? Put it up on the bench.' She moved aside, making room.

Chris couldn't take his eyes off Nick and Rose, on the edge of the crowd where there was more room. Nick had a style of his own; he didn't wriggle or bend or wave his arms about, but held himself erect yet supple, almost aloof. Except that every move he made, his intricate, unobtrusive footwork, closely involved his partner, though they hardly touched. And Rose followed suit, so that they were more together than if they had been in a clinch.

'He dances awfully well,' Rowan conceded. 'I couldn't do that in a million years. The way Rose follows.'

'She's good, too. It's pretty old hat, actually, jiving. Can you do the cha-cha?' He had learnt it at the fruit-picking camp.

'You know I can't. What is it anyway?'

'If it wasn't for this foot I'd show you.'

'It's too late now,' Rowan looked world-weary, 'I've missed out on dancing.'

'Oh, balls! It's practice you need. Above all someone you like dancing with. Anyone can dance, given a sense of rhythm.' An idea had begun to form itself: was it possible she could be persuaded to come up to London for the last week of her holidays?

He might have asked her there and then, but she interrupted him: 'I hope Nick knows what he's doing.'

'You've just said he was a super dancer.'

'Don't be a clot. You know very well what I mean – Rose.'

'I don't think it means much,' Chris chose his words carefully, evasively. 'Take the way they go on dancing. If you find someone you get on with the way he does with Rose, you want to keep together the whole evening. Like playing tennis.'

'I don't play tennis,' Rowan's coldness was a deserved response to his evasion.

'It must be tough on Mog.'

'He'll get over it. I don't suppose you'll be coming back.'

'I don't suppose we will. Well, I don't know why not. I might.' If I was asked, he left unsaid.

It was after midnight before they left Porthmawgan. Perhaps because of the drug taken earlier, or his earlier vicissitudes, or both, Chris slept as soon as he had dossed down on a folded sail, in the shelter of *Shearwater's* bulwarks, and didn't wake until they were rolling in to the Trewin River under Gwenan Head.

He was wearing his brother's thick sweater. Even having this pulled over his head and arms hadn't roused him. Nick was huddled up nearby, in his tee-shirt, with Rose nestling in the curve of his body. Chris was surprised by a sharp physical pain: he would have liked to be the one to harbour her, to feel her soft confiding warmth against him.

He glanced up at Rowan, standing at the tiller, vaguely guilty because of the strong pleasurable sensation the idea of Rose's body had stirred in him.

Standing beside Rowan, Mog looked back, out to sea. His face, in the light of dawn, was grey and miserable.

CHAPTER ELEVEN

Nick and Chris slept till lunch-time. On the kitchen table their mother had left instructions as to food, etc.

'They've gone off for their walk round the coast, then?'

'Yes. Taken *Seamouse* across to the village – aim to be back in time for Mog's birthday.'

Mog's birthday supper picnic was something of an occasion, occurring at the end of the holiday.

Chris got up and looked over the open half-door. 'A picnic? The weather's breaking.' Thunder clouds were massing in the south-west. He came back and sat down. 'I'm going over to Garrow this evening. Actually I'm going to ask Rowan if she'll come and stay. There's a week before school starts.'

His casual air was assumed: he was testing out the idea, unprecedented – neither of them, that he could remember, had ever asked a girl to stay.

'I shouldn't.' Nick, holding a knife between first and second fingers, was drumming lightly on the white scrubbed table. 'Rowan belongs here. I really shouldn't. It'd be a disaster.'

'Why should it be?'

'What'll you do with her? Hold hands in the front room? Walks in the cemetery – romantic place, the cemetery, weeping willows, dead chrysanths, specially at sunset.'

'Oh, stuff it! I'm serious.'

'I know you are. That's why I'm putting it to you in stark terms. Think of Rowan in that house.'

Chris considered their house, blowy nylon curtains, hallway polished every day, a copper ornament set precisely in the centre of the half-landing window. He followed Rowan into the cold, twin-bedded spare room, the bathroom with its candlewick toilet set. 'There's nothing wrong with the house. It's as big – bigger than Garrow Cottage. Aren't you being a bit snobby?'

'Not a question of snobbery – more what people are used to. Where they'd fit in. Rowan belongs here, same as Danny. She'd be bored stiff.'

'Danny doesn't think so. She wants Rowan to get away. Meet people. Actually, I thought we'd go into London – Westminster Abbey, Tower of London, go by boat down the river. Or Hampton Court. That's near us.'

Nick, now drumming with two knives, interrupted a complicated rhythm: 'Cost the earth, going round London. Besides, she's probably been to all those corny places. It's not as though she's never been there before. And "meeting people". The Youth Club? A C.N.D. rally in Hyde Park – have you thought of that? What d'you bet the Marshes are as Conservative as hell. Her Dad was a naval type, wasn't he? There's always the long-distance bike section of course.' (Chris belonged to the Young Socialists' Cycling Club.) 'Borrow a bike from the girl next door, down the Portsmouth Road to Guildford and beyond. Real matey, stopping at caffs, getting to know the lads. And the couples on tandems . . . She'll learn something worth while there. Life in the raw.'

Chris had ceased to listen, taken up by Nick's reference to C.N.D., his chief preoccupation since that first stupendous march to Aldermaston two years previously. Chris had not given it a thought since getting down here. It was as though something about the place had wiped out his entire life, made it seem unreal, unimportant. The idea of "opting out", as his parents would have said, which he had dismissed as impracticable, now seemed possible, indeed the only sensible course. He could get some sort of job, or if he could get a grant, go to a Tech. Combine the two – further education and earning enough to live on. If Jago could live at Otter Lodge, why not him? And it wasn't out of the question that Danny would let him stay as a paying guest with her. But Otter Lodge would be better – more independent.

'Actually,' he ventured casually, 'I might not come home. Not for good.'

'*Ectually,*' Nick got up, 'that's the third time you've used the word in the last couple of minutes. That's what I call snobbery. And "jolly D", and "Thanks most *awfully*" when a bloke hands you a fag, as though he was doing you a favour. Rowan and Danny don't "ectually" you all over the place.'

'Aren't you being snobby in reverse? If it's the Travises you're thinking about, you see more of them than I do. Anyway I don't believe they say "actually" much, or any of the other things you say I say.'

'Come to think of it, they don't, noticeably. I can't think where you did pick up this crappy talk. Some master, I bet, at that grotty school, and now it's coming out like a rash – over-excitement at breaking into a new social environment. To get back to the point I was making, what's snobby about it is, it's not the way you talk at home. Thank God.'

Chris had had enough of being brought up by hand by his brother.

'You're more socially insecure than I am.' He was fitting Nick's remarks in with his performance before taking a girl out. 'Your Cambridge mate says all those things, I shouldn't wonder.' Chris knew the man's name perfectly well.

'*Ectually,* he doesn't. And if he did, I wouldn't.' Nick yawned and stretched: 'I'm going back to bed. I shall be out late, in case I'm still asleep when you leave. I'm taking the car – giving Rose a night out in Porthmawgan. There's an Italian restaurant. And a jazz club, surprisingly enough. Not bad, either.'

'Why *surprising*?' Chris was defending Porthmawgan from what seemed condescension.

'You *are* picking on everything – better have a kip yourself after yesterday. Surprising because jazz isn't popular – old hat, isn't it? You're the young, swinging generation. And Rose, you may have noticed, jives superbly.'

93

'Yeah, well. You've always said jazz is something to listen to, not for dancing.'

'You get everything wrong. When you get a kid who can dance like Rose . . .' They were standing at the foot of the stairs.

'That's another thing. What about Rose?'

Nick's face went rigid: '*What* about Rose?'

'She *doesn't* live down here, does she. I mean, she'll want to see you after we get back.'

'Rose,' Nick quietly weighed every word, 'is-becoming-a-bit-of-a-bore.' He put a foot on the stairs. 'Understand this: she's a nice kid, a smashing kid for her age. In two or three years' time, if she makes it without some sort of disaster, she'll be more than smashing. Right now, she could be a menace. She has a rotten time at home – her Mum's in a bin, and one of her young brothers – she wouldn't tell me what happened to him. Naturally she latches on to all and sundry, me, for example. Taking her sailing, giving her a good time like tonight – where's the harm in that? Nothing but good. What more do you expect me to do? Prise her off with a cold chisel? Once back home she'll forget the whole episode. And if she doesn't, it's hardly my concern, is it? Well, *is* it?'

With a dry cough, he turned and went upstairs.

Chris was left leaning over the half-door. He ached all over, and his foot hurt. Distant thunder rumbled; steady rain fell. There was no wind.

Turning to his own concerns, Chris tried to sort them out. As so often, the kind of talk he had had with his brother had left him in a muddle, issues left unresolved. Rowan . . . they'd been talking about her as though she was some sort of animal, an otter, a seal, that couldn't live out of its environment. Or Nick had. He now realised that he himself couldn't easily imagine her away from Garrow. And yet – what utter balls! This was at least as unrealistic as his urge to cut loose and live down here. He'd go over to Garrow, he decided, after tea, and ask her.

A door slammed. Feet slapped along the wet lane. Tosh, wearing yellow oilies and sou-wester. As she passed, he called out: 'Super time we had!'

She gave him a quick look, without slowing down, and flushed. Staring straight ahead she ignored him. Her glance had been reproachful, puzzled, then angry.

Chris felt terrible. Her coolness was understandable; but what was it to do with him, if Rose had gone off Tosh's brother?

Bloody unfair, he concluded, taking the stairs slowly, a step at a time.

When he woke up, the rain had stopped. He lay for a time, refreshed, contemplating the watery sunshine that came and went, slanting through the little window. From its position, time must be getting on. Nick had left.

Hunger was what got him on his feet. He made himself a filling meal, mostly out of tins, went into the bathroom, washed, and forced himself to peel off last night's dirty plaster on his heel. The burst blister looked disgusting. He might as well try Mrs Trewin's remedy. He drew on his sneakers, put a tin of Elastoplast in his pocket and made for the shore.

Halfway to Garrow Point, seeing a convenient rock in deep enough water, he waded out, settled himself and submerged his foot. Relaxed after his sleep, lulled by gurgles and plops, he took an occasional look at his heel, whiter and cleaner, crinkled by immersion in seawater. Mrs Trewin's folk-lore remedy seemed to be working.

He turned over in his mind the talk with Nick. "Ectually" . . .

Another puzzling aspect of Nick's life which often pre-occupied him was his being so extremely left-wing. Dangerously so, it seemed to Chris, considering his clearly defined business interests. His friend was just as bad, according to Nick himself, having belonged at Cambridge to a Trotskyist group. The Young Socialists were forever being warned about these subversive saboteurs, intent on "infiltrating"

95

decent, British democratic organisations.

Chris had once put it to Nick – how could he reconcile his business life, his declared aim of "getting to the top", with his anti-capitalist beliefs? And wasn't his job endangered?

'No problem,' Nick had replied. 'For one thing one has one's principles; and unless you bore the pants off the people you work with they accept you for what you are, providing you do a decent job. Besides, it's a matter of enlightened self-interest – understanding the system, the social set-up, puts you one jump ahead of the poor sods in the City who are floundering about more and more feebly. No doubt of it, capitalism is on the verge of crumbling from within. And when it does, we shall be ready to take over.'

Chris was sure there were flaws in Nick's theory – he could think of some himself. But up to now he hadn't met anyone who could equal or surpass his brother's grasp of affairs. Jack Travis, he'd be interesting to talk to. And now there wouldn't be time.

He was roused by a shout from the shore. It was Mog, and he saw at once what he must be shouting about: the tide was coming in, fast enough for him to wade back up to his thighs.

'Thanks a lot,' he said, hopping over the wet sand because he didn't want to put his clean heel down. He sat down to examine it, feeling in his pocket for the Elastoplast. The spaniel came up and sniffed his foot.

'Here,' Mog held out a handkerchief, 'it won't stick unless the skin's dry.'

Chris looked at him gratefully, not so much for the handkerchief as for Mog's not cutting him as Tosh appeared to have done.

The two walked along the shore in silence, Mog occasionally throwing a stick for his dog to retrieve, picking up a shell and dropping it, or chucking a flat pebble over the water.

A livid, yellowish light made the shore and the woods strange, unfriendly. The storm was not done with; everything waited for more. The curving shore seemed desolate, strewn with blackish objects.

Suddenly Mog said with quiet certainty, 'I'm going to marry Rose.'

Chris, after a moment's silence, replied, 'People hardly ever do marry the people they think they're going to.'

'We've always been going to. Since we were kids. It's been settled for a long time.'

Referring to what must be in both their minds, Chris said, 'We shan't be coming back, I shouldn't think. At least, I might. But on my own.'

'That's what I thought.'

So as not to pursue the subject, Chris asked, 'D'you ever feel you're being rail-roaded through life? On at one end and off at the other?'

'You mean, your whole life?'

'Lord, no. School and that. Home. Day after day. What you're booked to do next.'

'I don't think I do. But I know what you mean. My people are pretty decent. I suppose they're a bit sick that I don't want to try for university, but they don't go on about it.'

'Aren't you going to?'

'No. They'll let me leave school when I've got three A-levels – one of them in Art, so it shouldn't be too difficult. Not that Art's an easy option; but I'm quite good at it. As I say, after that I shall go to France. There's a film director I've got a chance to work for. It'll take ages, of course. I shall be lucky if I get as far as being clapper-boy.'

'You're lucky knowing what you want to do.' How would Rose fit in? Pretty well, he supposed. She would be good at fitting in. 'Mum's frightfully ambitious for me. Wants me to be a teacher. Can't leave it alone. Actually – I mean, in fact – I wouldn't so much mind if I could be like your Dad. He *did* go to university?'

97

'Yes. But you don't have to. You get more money, I think, if you do.'

'I like him quite a lot. I bet he's a good teacher. Fair and – and not bloody-minded.'

'He can be bloody-minded at home. Takes it out on Mother. She weathers it – says he can't let off steam at school, specially now he's a Head.'

They trudged along in the loose sand. Summer lightning flickered and sheeted the skies, moving from one quarter to another; it was all round them, and getting closer.

'Women have a rotten time,' Mog remarked.

Chris, thinking of his own mother, supposed they did. Forever doing things they didn't choose to, like sitting in pubs drinking endless shandies.

'The storm will break soon.' Mog sniffed. 'You can smell the sulphur in the air.'

'Let's hope so.' Pressure was beginning to build up in Chris's head. 'I can almost feel my hair crackle.'

Silence followed.

Then Chris resumed, 'What you said about women. Depends who they are, wouldn't you think? Danny and Rowan – they seem to do more or less what they want. At least they're pretty good at not doing things they don't want to.'

After some thought Mog said, 'That's what makes them so super to be with. Their not wanting other people to do things all the time.'

'I should have thought your family were pretty easy-going?'

'Is anyone's? Things get pretty tense, specially on holiday. Not so bad when one's young – perhaps one notices it more. I'm thinking of getting a holiday job in France next summer.'

They had come to the foot of the rock where the rope hung down.

'But won't you always want to come back?'

'How do I know what I shall feel?' Mog hit the rock

98

savagely with the flat of his hand.

Chris twisted the rope on and off his arm like a snake. Not wanting to leave Mog, hoping he would come, he said, 'I'm going up to the cottage now.' He swung on the rope. 'I might want to come back and see Danny, wherever I was, specially if something awful had happened. She's the most extraordinary person. It's not so much what she says. . . .'

'It's what she doesn't say.'

'Coming?'

Mog shook his head.

At the top Chris looked back, watched the dejected figure striding away, his dog at his heels, growing smaller with distance.

CHAPTER TWELVE

Lightning split the sky: and with the first thundercrack rain fell, thudding on the leaves, drenching him before he had run fifty yards. A sudden wind rushed through treetops, racked the woods. His energy released by the storm, he ran through the swaying trees, abandoned, exultant, past the boathouse and up the path, now a running stream, to the cottage.

At the edge of the lawn he stopped, drawing breath from the bottom of his lungs. The storm had passed over as suddenly as it had come; but the rain was unabated. Across the veridian grass, cutting the unearthly half-light, light from an opened door shone on him, still as a rock under a waterfall.

'Who's that?' Danny called. 'Chris! Come in quick – I'm already soaked.'

He stood just inside the door, a pool forming round him on the stone floor.

Danny fetched a towel: 'You'd better strip. Rub yourself down while I get dry clothes.'

She brought him down a thick sweater and a pair of faded pink sailcloth trousers, and put a match to the kindling under the logs in the fireplace. He towelled his hair and his top half, peeling off his jeans while she finished what she had been doing at the sink.

She came and switched on a reading lamp by the blazing hearth. 'I'll make some coffee.' She draped his wet things over a clothes-horse near the fire.

He sank into the roll-collared sweater, the deep-cushioned armchair. The sweater smelt of newly-washed wool. The trousers were too big at the waist, too short in the leg; there was something pleasantly sexy about wearing Danny's clothes. Rain hissed on the huge granite hearth; if you put your head up the flue you could see the stars. Books lined the recesses; some were leatherbound, their gilt titles catching the lamplight.

She brought a tray and sat down opposite.

'You made it after all, yesterday?'

He told her about the Rolls and Mrs Trewin and Jago. Nothing pleased him more than making Danny laugh, unless it was making Rowan laugh, which was that much harder.

'I really came to see Rowan.'

'She's in the stable tending Snapdragon. In one of her "states". Result of yesterday, I dare say.'

'Is that what she does when she's feeling bloody-minded – holes up in the stable? I go for long bike rides.' He leant forward. 'I came to ask her something. D'you think she'd come to London for a few days before term starts?'

'I'd like it if she would. You'd better ask her.'

'What about the boats?'

'I can manage. It's a bit of a ploy, the boats, only don't tell her I said so. Not that she isn't awfully useful; I'd find it difficult to carry on without her. But it makes a copper-bottomed excuse for getting out of other things. Go and ask her now. I'm off to an early bed. You can get your clothes in the morning. Oh, and put this oilie over your shoulders.'

The pony nearly filled the small stable, lit by a storm lantern. Rowan looked round as he entered and turned back to feeding Snapdragon a warm bran mash.

The animal shifted; Chris, cautiously skirting his broad rump, sat down on a bale of straw. Rowan's transistor played softly, tuned in to Radio Luxembourg. Rain drummed on the tin roof.

'He's not feeling too good. And thunderstorms upset him terribly.'

She had mucked out the stable and put down fresh straw; the rack was filled with hay.

Chris settled back into the straw bales, savouring the

sweet, pungent odour of the stable; the radio was playing "Living Doll". Rowan, absorbed, scraped the last of the bran mash from the bucket, and Snapdragon, sated, withdrew his head and nuzzled into her hand. She stroked his nose rhythmically, lovingly, her hair falling forward.

The rain had almost ceased; no sound broke the silence except for the radio, or when Snapdragon shifted a hoof, quivering slightly under his blanket, exhaling through widening nostrils what must surely be a sigh of contentment.

Neither Chris nor Rowan felt the need to talk. It crossed Chris's mind that this was what marriage could be like.

After a while, growing sleepy, he remembered what he had come for. 'I wondered if you'd like to come to London for a few days before term starts?'

Rowan, herself half asleep, raised her head, surprised, putting her hair back behind one ear. 'I don't know. Would it be a good idea?'

'If you think so.'

'Later on, perhaps? I'll think about it.'

He leant forward a little. 'It will be so long before I see you. I've got so used to coming here, seeing you every day.' He had not meant to say so much, not known, even, that the thought was there.

At this, she bent forward to pick a spoon off the ground; impossible to tell what effect his words had had on her, if he had gone too far in breaching her reserve.

'It wouldn't do now – I couldn't leave Mother with the boats.'

'I asked her – she said she could manage, she'd like you to come.'

Before the words were out he knew he had made a mistake.

She tossed her hair back. 'I wish she wouldn't interfere.'

'She interferes less than anyone else I know. Specially when you've got no father. Would you tell me,' he couldn't help asking, 'I've always wondered, and there might not be

another chance. What happened to him? What did he do?
I know he was in the Navy.'

'We don't know what happened to him. He just never
came back after one of his trips. Quite early in 1944. He
used to go off, you know –'

'Off where?'

'What he did was secret. But Mother guessed, more or
less. He – and of course there were others too – used to go
over to France, sometimes to bring people back when they
needed to escape, sometimes for other reasons that we don't
know about. You see, having sailed here all his life, and
across the Channel, he knew the French coast and the Channel Islands as well as he knew Cornwall. Could find his way
into any creek in the dark. Celia Travis's brother was with
him. He never came back either, that last time. And Rose
– Rose had an uncle in Falmouth. He got back after some
earlier raid, but wounded. He died soon after.'

'I wish I'd known your Dad. And you must.'

'We talked about him a lot, specially when I was little.'

Now wide awake, she came and stood over him: 'Rose,'
she said, suddenly severe, 'I suppose your brother knows
what he's doing?'

Taken off balance, Chris replied evasively, 'What do you
mean, exactly?'

'You know what I mean. He's taken her dancing tonight,
hasn't he? He must be pretty keen on her; only he doesn't
let her know it. I think he ought to, not knowing makes
her feel so awful.'

Chris, floundering: 'What do you expect him to say?
Why should she feel so awful? She likes being with him a
lot. And he's giving her a good time, isn't he?'

'*A good time?*' Rowan's contempt stung him, on Nick's
behalf. Chris stood up; they were very close to one another
and Rowan stepped back, hitting Snapdragon on his flank
to get out of the way.

'What's wrong with that?' He was talking like his brother
now.

'*Wrong?* You think that's all Rose is after – a "good time"? She's in love with him.'

'She's certainly fairly crazy about him. She makes that more than obvious.' Chris, too, was angry, mostly because he agreed with Rowan. But his brother had a case, there was something to be said on his side.

'Get out!' Her low, controlled voice was worse than if she had screamed. 'You come here upsetting people, making them miserable – there's Mog, too, don't forget – and think you can go away saying, oh that's fine, we've given them a good time!'

'Leave me out of it.' Chris stood his ground. 'To Nick, Rose is just a nice kid . . .'

'That's what makes it particularly beastly of him, her being so much younger. You'll be telling me in a minute how "kind" Nick is – you're always going on about it.'

'He is, too. Shut up and listen. That's how he thinks of Rose – a nice kid. And he'd be a bastard if he didn't, if he made a pass at her, I mean, *really* did. Well, wouldn't he?'

Rowan's face was stony.

'Nick doesn't think of her that way. If he wanted to make a girl he'd go for someone more his own age. Or older.' Dismissing Mrs Trewin from his mind, Chris tried to think of the nicest older woman imaginable. 'He'd go for someone like – well, like Danny.'

'My *mother?*' Rowan turned away and picked up the empty bucket. 'You must be mad as well as disgusting.'

Chris wrenched open the door, which stuck.

Walking across the lawn, he thought: That's it. No London. No Rowan, come to that. In his anger it was satisfying to have Nick's advice confirmed – her coming to London would have been disastrous.

The air was fresh, the stars as softly brilliant as ever. From the edge of the woods he could still smell the verbena bush that grew by Danny's door.

CHAPTER THIRTEEN

'Letter came for you yesterday, Dad. I stuck it on the mantelpiece by the clock,' Chris said.

The Mitchells were sitting outside before lunch, in sunshine as strong as ever, though there were signs that the long, hot spell was coming to an end. Nick, who had been out all night, had got back in time to meet *Seamouse* on the hard. Their parents' walk round the Lizard had been a success: no better way of rounding off a memorable holiday.

'A letter – who from? No one knows we're here.'

'That's what I thought. Got a Leicester postmark.'

'But we don't know anyone from there.'

Chris fetched the letter, and his father opened it.

Mrs Mitchell held out a hand: 'Well, go on – what's it about?'

But her husband, resisting for once, held it away from her.

'It's from a furniture manufacturer.' His face, already brick-red from wind and sun, had grown darker. 'Signed by the Managing Director. They're offering me a job. Want me to go for an interview, at least.'

His hand shook as he handed the letter over.

His wife read it, glanced at Nick. 'You fixed this?'

'Sort of. It was such a hundred-to-one-chance I didn't want to say anything. I remembered this bloke I work with has an uncle running this factory in Leicester. You'll think it over, I suppose? It's not what you've been used to, Dad. Mass-produced stuff, see it everywhere. And it'll mean moving.'

His father got up. 'More beer, I think, don't you?'

Chris jumped up, seeing his father holding on to the doorpost: 'I'll get it.' But Mr Mitchell shook his head.

Nick's mother looked at him. 'That was good of you.'

And that, for the Mitchell family, was all that needed saying.

Chris felt let down in two ways: a release from tension shared by them all; but also a sense of anti-climax. He had had an unfamiliar impulse – he had wanted to hug his Dad, which he hadn't done since being in the Junior school. He would have liked to hug everyone, Nick above all. He would have liked his mother to hug their father; she had gone indoors after him and perhaps she was doing just that, though he doubted it since they didn't normally embrace in front of their children, and he couldn't envisage their private behaviour.

Chris also felt mean, since a sizeable part of his relief had been the realisation that his father wasn't going to be at home all day during the holidays – pretty unimportant compared with the main issue, his being able to look forward to a working future.

'Gosh!' he contented himself with saying to his brother, 'that was about the best thing you've ever done!'

Nick, having run out of cigars, was rolling himself a fag, moistening a finger to draw out a cigarette paper. 'It was a damn near run thing.'

'And keeping it under your hat all this time!'

'What was the point of telling anyone – even you? As I said, it was a hundred-to-one-chance. God, though, I'm glad it came off! You'll quite like Leicester. They've got a good education system, sixth-form colleges, I think, but you won't find it all that different.'

'I might not be going.'

'What d'you mean, not going? Of course you'll have to. Where d'you think you're going to live? Apart from practicalities, they'll need settling in – imagine those two on their own, new job, new environment – they depend on us being around more than most couples, or haven't you noticed it?' He paused to light his fag, thin and droopy, fringed at the end. After several spent matches he resumed, 'That was crap what I just said. It's not up to you how they make out. Only I don't see you can avoid staying at home till you finish school. What had you in mind? Not –'

'No. I wasn't going to suggest moving in with you. I've just got the feeling I want to get out and be on my own. At least, I had . . .'

While Nick talked, Chris had time to review his scene with Rowan last night which, till now, he had managed not to think about. The full significance of what had passed between them now hit him: "You must be mad as well as disgusting". One thing was certain: she wouldn't want to see him again. Nor would he want to see her. What he had said, trying to explain Nick's attitude, had been reasonable – as clear as he could make it considering the complexity of Nick's affairs.

So now, of course, there was no question of his trying out the plan to stay down here; and he saw, anyway, that it would never have worked.

'You're absolutely right,' he said. 'I had an idea – but I can see now that it was crazy. It's this place, don't you think? Makes you do crazy things, things, I mean that you'd know were crazy if you were anywhere else. In fact they'd never come up.'

Nick looked guarded. 'I'm not sure I catch your drift. I don't think I'm doing anything I wouldn't do elsewhere.'

Their mother, coming out with a tray of drinks and sandwiches, interrupted: 'They even offer to arrange temporary accommodation! Supposing he gets the job, of course – and he will. And with my work I should be very unlucky not to get fixed up in a local hospital.'

Her husband had come out and now sat back, swirling his beer round, staring into the glass.

'You're happy about going,' Nick asked, 'you're sure you want the job?'

'What d'you think, son? It takes some getting used to. I'd given up all hope – didn't stand a chance, at my age.'

But you might have tried a bit harder, Chris thought,

refusing the offer of a sandwich: 'I'm not hungry, thanks. See you later.'

Ignoring his mother's objection he walked away in the opposite direction to Garrow.

He found himself in the lane leading up to Trewin House. Over the gate he saw Jago at work in the vegetable garden, clearing the jungle, a battle which, today, he seemed to be winning.

'Could I give you a hand?'

'I wouldn't half mind.'

Jago handed over his hatchet and Chris, stripping off his tee-shirt, took over.

An hour's vigorous slashing followed, using all his strength under full sunlight.

At last Jago returned: 'Hold it, hadn't you better?' He had to repeat himself before Chris heard, and let his arm fall.

'Here,' Jago held out a mug of tea.

'Thanks, but I ought to be going – there's this picnic. What's the time?'

Jago looked at the sun. 'Around tea-time, I should say. You'd better cool off, hadn't you? You look like an over-ripe plum.'

Chris stretched himself on the grass, drinking the tea in gulps. His sweat-drenched body dried in the sun, his heart stopped pounding.

'Just what the doctor ordered.'

Chris nodded, aware that Jago's reference was to the need for slashing, not the tea.

'Thanks a lot.'

He vaulted over the gate and ran all the way down to the cottages.

Everyone was on the shore; he joined them in time to see *Shearwater* tearing up the river, Danny towing the two girls on water-skis, their hair flying behind them.

'Oh, boy!' his father was heard to exclaim, 'was that a sight to remember!'

Danny made a wide circle and slowed down as near as she could get to the beach at half-tide. Those who wanted to have a go swam out. Chris ran back to the cottage for his swimming-trunks, returning as Nick and Mog, both expert, disappeared up-river, skidding this way and that.

Two by two the skiers were helped into the boat, but Chris still hung back.

'Come on!' Tosh had swum back for him. Chris took this as a sign that she regretted her coldness yesterday. In his touchy mood, he might even have imagined it.

'I've never tried it.'

'Well, try it now, only hurry. I'm no good either, but it's a gorgeous feeling when you manage to stay up.'

Chris saw her point when, after a few attempts, he managed to keep his balance for a few exhilarating seconds.

He levered himself into the waiting boat as Rowan offered him a sopping towel: 'Not much good, I'm afraid, but you'll have to swim back anyway.'

As the party dived in, leaving the girls to go back with Danny, she called to him, 'See you this evening.'

From her manner you might think nothing had happened between them.

Well, thought Chris, breaking into a powerful crawl, it happened to me all right and she needn't think I'm going to pretend it didn't.

Back at the cottages, preparations were already in hand for the picnic. All doors stood open; there was much running in and out, lending, borrowing, checking and re-checking.

'Like D-day,' Mr Mitchell commented during an interval for refreshment when anyone who happened to be un-occupied sat outside sampling the drink intended for the evening.

The sun was low when the little fleet of motorboats and dinghies, headed by Danny in *Shearwater*, set out for Mirren Quay, above Otter Lodge.

This great granite, grass-covered structure, dating from

the time when the river was navigable for trading vessels, was big enough to accommodate everyone. Hampers were unpacked, wine bottles lowered into the water to cool, and Ben Pernel and Jack Travis, in charge of the cooking, set up their rough iron spit.

Mog's younger brother was practising casting flies with Mog's new rod, a little way upstream.

Those who wanted to swam. The water, from travelling over the sun-baked mudflats, was warm; but the sharpness of autumn was in the air, and leaves, brown, yellow, crimson, floated down at the turn of the tide.

Others had set themselves to unpacking and spreading out the feast. There were cries of: 'Watch it!' and: 'You oaf – take your foot off those pasties!'

Someone cried, 'Drinking water – we want more water. Who's got the key of Otter Lodge?'

'Rose has.'

'Ro-o-se – got the key of Otter Lodge?'

A cauldron had been set to boil; and Ben produced the biggest, blackest frying-pan that anyone had ever seen.

'He found it down at Gwenan. Must be off some ship.'

'How would it float?' Chris asked. But no one heard. He was sitting a little apart, where one side of the quay had collapsed into a cascade of granite setts and boulders. Here Mr Mitchell and Mulley, the Travis granny, had found comfortable seats; between them they had taken over babies and toddlers leaving their mothers free, 'off the hook', as Mr Mitchell put it.

His wife's Guider training was proving its worth as cook's assistant: 'Lovely – sausages and potatoes!'

'Not just *that*,' Delia Travis stuck a hairpin into her wet curls, skewering them to the top of her head. 'Ben always does something special for Mog's birthday – over-ambitious, sometimes. But we can always fall back on the spuds and bangers.'

'Where's Nick?' Mr Mitchell looked about him.

'Fetching more water from Otter Lodge with Rose.'

The flames had subsided, leaving red-hot stones and embers. With abandon, Ben emptied half a sack of rice into the boiling cauldron, and a dollop of butter into the frying-pan, drawn away from the heat. 'Unwrap that pack of crab-meat, could you?'

'My goodness!' Mrs Mitchell's admiration was tempered with mistrust: 'Not *crab pilaff*, on a spit like that, out in the open?'

'Herbs!' Ben cried, and his assistant had them to hand, likewise the other ingredients, split almonds, paprika . . .

Jack Travis had drawn up the net of wine bottles; corks were drawn, enamel mugs clunked, Mog's health was drunk.

Mog himself responded with an effort; then came over to Chris with a bottle and two mugs: 'Better make sure of it before they drink the lot.'

The two boys sat in silence, neither content. Rose and Nick were so long fetching the water. As for Chris, he was accustoming himself to an unhappy explanation of Rowan's friendly behaviour after the water-skiing: if she could go on as if nothing had happened, it must be because he was of no importance to her, she hadn't given her parting words last night another thought.

'I think,' Mog poured the last of the wine into Chris's mug, 'I shall do A-level Geography.'

'Why?'

'I reckon you'd need it to become an explorer. Expeditions take expert cameramen.'

'Not a bad idea. Where? The Amazon?'

'South Pole, if possible. No women.'

'They can be the most ball-aching bore. I bet those sausages are ready.'

'I can't understand them. Can't ever be sure what they want, what they're thinking.'

'The thing is,' Chris spoke confidently, fortified by the wine on an empty stomach, 'not to think about them. The moment they think you're *not* thinking about them they start thinking about you.'

A tremendous rumpus had started up on the other side of the quay.

'I see what you meant when you said your holidays could be rather tense – so many people, such a lot of kids.'

There had already been minor disputes, a cut foot, a squabble over a rock-pool, a lost ball. But now screams indicated some major disaster. Mog and Chris hurried over.

'I told you not to bring that bloody rod!' Jack was roaring.

'It's all right,' Mrs Mitchell had taken over. 'The hook's not in her eye –'

'It might have been.'

'It's in her hair. Come on over here, you, and hold that rod carefully.' She deftly disentangled the hook.

Mog retrieved his rod. His brother, in tears, kept repeating, 'I told her not to come so near. I *told* her . . .'

'It's always like this at picnics,' Mog complained to Chris when they were settled once more, this time with two cardboard platefuls of charred sausages, baked, blackened potatoes and a generous helping of crab pilaff, to be washed down with beer and cider: 'Every year something goes wrong.'

'I like it. I wish we had a big family, lots of cousins. And your uncle, cooking this stuff on a picnic. It's luscious.'

'Too special by half. We should have eaten ages ago. And the midges – terrible. They always are.'

'Have a fag.' It was Nick who spoke. He and Rose had come to sit just above them.

'No, thanks.'

'They'll keep the midges off.'

Rose wouldn't have one, but took alternate puffs of Nick's.

'Isn't is super,' she bent to talk to Chris, 'Mog's birthday picnic? Sometimes we have fireworks. Nick says he might fix something special. But he won't say what.'

'Wait till it's dark,' Nick said.

'That shouldn't be long – look at those clouds coming up.'

Rowan came round bearing a plate-shaped basket of fruit. Nick took it from her before Chris could offer. Above him, the two girls were quietly conferring: 'I've got my flute,' Rowan said. 'We could do the Glück.'

'All right. I'll get my recorder.' Rose slipped away. Mog, in spite of his resolution, followed her.

Rowan's voice, behind Chris, was low: 'I didn't mean what I said last night. It was vicious. That's Mother's word – she says I can be vicious, but I hardly ever am. Never like last night.'

'I didn't think you did mean it. At least, I hoped you wouldn't when you thought about it. Then I thought, perhaps it wasn't important enough for you to bother – to remember what you'd said.'

'Oh –' she caught her breath.

Neither dared to move, to break the understanding between them.

Rose and Mog came back.

'We always end up playing something,' Rose said, 'it seems a bit silly, but they like it – Mulley and the others.'

As the girls rowed Mog's boat across the river and anchored in the black shadows of the trees opposite, preparations were made for departure while there was light enough to see.

Westward, clouds were massing, reflecting the fire of the vanished sun, shedding a furnace light on fields, woods and water. That light caught the wing of a heron flying upstream to the heronry.

Flute and recorder sounded clear across the water; Chris knew what they were playing, and was to hear it many times afterwards. But always and forever the theme, telling how Orpheus, looking back, loses Eurydice, would bring him back in memory to this time, this place.

In the silence that followed, no one moved. Then a slight sound behind him made Chris turn his head.

Mrs Trewin and Jago were standing where Nick and Rose had sat. He turned back, not knowing how long they had been there. Not having come by boat, they must have walked down through the woods from Mirren Farm.

He heard Mog's boat grounding on the shore and ran down to catch the painter, hoping it was too dark for Rose to look up and see Mrs Trewin. At the same time he heard a boat engine start up from the quay: *Seamouse*, and Nick, just visible, standing at the tiller. He seemed to be circling aimlessly around, well clear of both shores; what could he be about?

Then, as *Seamouse* roared shorewards, the water behind her burst into flames, circles, zig-zags, figures-of-eight!

The sight was so staggering, so startlingly spectacular, that a second or two were needed to take it in. Then followed a burst of clapping, cries of incredulity and admiration not unmixed with a ground bass of disapproval.

Avoiding the crowded quay, Nick ran the boat keel-deep into the mud.

'That's what he wanted the petrol for,' cried Rose. 'What a glorious end to the evening!'

Danny, at Chris's elbow, muttered, 'Damn dangerous! If he's done no more than blister the paint he'll be lucky.'

As Nick passed Chris said, 'You must be pissed!'

'Tight as a tick.' Nick, making for the path above, did not stop.

With the dying of the flames, darkness settled over the water. Boat parties were organised, hampers lowered over the quayside, embers stamped out, children woke, cried and slept again as they were carried to the boats.

'Chris!' Mrs Mitchell's voice overrode the clamour.

'Here, I'm down here.' Chris was doing his best to push *Seamouse* clear of the mud and keep her afloat. Nick, instead of taking her back to the quay where there was deep water, once the danger of fire was over, had disappeared.

She scrambled down, beginning at once, 'You realise you haven't done your packing –'

'Stuff that! Give me a hand, or we shall be grounded for the night. *Seamouse* is a keelboat, don't forget.'

Together they pushed her sternmost into the water:
'Now – get aboard!'

As *Seamouse* was freed from the mud, his mother responded with all her agility, levering herself over the gunwale and seizing an oar ready to push off into deeper water.
'Get the engine going,' she cried, 'we'll get home on our
own. Dad and Nick can find their own way back – there's
heaps of boats. It's about tomorrow.'

When Chris had set the boat on course, she shouted in
his ear, over the engine noise, 'It's your bike. You realise
you'll have to come back with us?'

Chris had given no more thought to his damaged bike.

'It's so like you to go off the way you did this afternoon,
without giving a thought to tomorrow. You don't think
we're going to pay your fare? Let alone what your bike
would cost extra. You and Nick will have to squeeze into
the back, or better still you and me, as Nick will be sharing
the driving. He says if you take the wheels off we might get
the bike and the luggage on the rack. That's why I want
you home. We've got to make an early start – you'll have
to do the job tonight, in the kitchen where there's light.'

'If the bike's to lie flat I'll have to take the pedals off,
you realize?'

When they tied up on the pulley-hauley Chris murmured,
'What about returning *Seamouse* to the Marshes?'

'Never mind about that. Get cracking on your bike.'

There would be no saying goodbye to Danny and Rowan.

At last, the bike packed flat on the floor, Chris went up
to bed, pausing to look over the half-door before shutting
it. The noise of the returning party had subsided. Lights
were out all along the row.

Slipping out of his salt-encrusted jeans he lay on his bed,
hands behind his head.

The familiar sound of hooves had him sitting bolt up-
right. Rowan! She had come to say goodbye after all. He

scrabbled for his jeans in the dark, rolled over Nick's empty bed and was out in the lane as Rowan reached the cottage, riding Snapdragon bareback.

'Rose hasn't come back. I woke up and she wasn't there. Is she with you?'

'No.'

'She said she'd wait for Nick – borrowed Mog's boat. Nick had gone to put the petrol can back, she said. We – Mother and I – were the last to leave and Nick still hadn't turned up. But you know Rose when she's set on something.'

They both looked towards the hard. The night was not clear; but the waning moon, smouldering behind thin, layered cloud, gave light enough to show that Mog's boat was not on the pulley-hauley.

The pony shifted and Rowan patted his neck.

'I suppose you think I'm making a fuss?' She spoke as though this had just occurred to her. 'If Rose is with Nick . . . *if* she is, that makes it all right, I suppose you'd think?' Her voice had hardened. Clearly, for her, it was not all right.

'I don't think you are fussing.' He was thinking of Mrs Trewin's brief appearance at the party. Before he could go on Rowan continued in a rush, 'She's been so queer lately, you get used to Rose's moods but sometimes it's a bit frightening, not anything you could put your finger on, even Mother's noticed it, and you see we do know each other so awfully well . . . The moment I woke up I thought: something's happened to Rose. Something awful.'

Chris, as though he, too, knew Rose's mind said, 'I'm pretty sure I know where she is – where she might be.' If anything terrible were to happen, Rose had said, this is where I'd want to be. The most terrible thing he could think of was her coming on Nick and Mrs Trewin together at Otter Lodge. For this reason alone he didn't want Rowan there. 'I'll bring her back safely, I promise. But I must go on my own. It'll be all right. I'm almost certain she's all right.'

'She'd better be.'

Not giving her time to stop him, he shouldered the out-board motor leaning against the cottage wall, ran down to the hard, boarded *Seamouse* and headed up-river.

He had no clear idea why he wanted so much to search for Rose alone. That she was his responsibility, because of Nick's involvement, he was in no doubt. But he had begun to feel a deeper link between them; if she was in trouble he wanted to be with her.

There were several possibilities, the worst being her dis-covery of Nick and Mrs Trewin together. The more he thought about this the less likely it seemed, for several reasons. But he was becoming less and less surprised by people's behaviour, whatever their age.

As he turned up Mirren Creek, mats of seaweed floated swiftly by. At first sight his stomach turned over: the idea of Rose's drowning herself only now came to him. She was so strange and passionate and insecure.

The bows nosed a soft object: in horror he leant out and grabbed as the thing floated past, a corpse-like shape of canvas and rope. Recovering his balance he seized the tiller and righted the boat's course, but missed the little inlet at Otter Lodge, only realising his mistake when Mirren Quay showed up ahead. Going about he tried to recall any land-mark; there was the clump of tall beeches where the tree-house was. But would it show up? Not against rising ground.

Making once more for Mirren Quay, he rammed the keel in the muddy bottom as the granite side loomed up, splashed and struggled through water and mud, making the painter fast on an iron ring.

The path from the quay to Otter Lodge ran inland, skirting a miniature lagoon; this much he remembered. Feeling his way from tree to tree in the darkest parts, hurrying onward where the branches opened to the sky, sliding on mud, once rolling down a bank of brambles, he had begun to think himself lost when he came to an open space: the hollow where the Lascar seamen were buried.

Soon he stood before Otter Lodge. Chris stood without moving, suddenly more afraid than ever before. He had been so sure he would find Rose here. But if she were not? He had no more ideas. He put his head round one of the glass doors and quietly spoke her name. Listening to the silence he pulled it open. Used to darkness he saw the mattresses. And on one a humped shape.

'Rose.' He knelt beside her. She was lying face downwards. He touched her shoulder. He tried to turn her towards him but she was as limp as a rag doll and much colder. He touched her cheek. It was dry. Her bare feet were icy.

Fetching a blanket he wrapped it round her and tried to take her into his arms to warm her. He pulled her half on to his knees where he knelt and began to hold and rock her. He stroked her hair out of her eyes.

'Oh, Rose!' he murmured. 'Rose, Rose.' As though he were rocking a child.

At last, to his relief, she began to cry. Dry sobs at first that shook her so that he held her tighter, then passionate weeping. She reached up out of the blanket and put her arms round his neck, as though he was dragging her out of the sea. He began to kiss her wet cheeks, her hair, her eyelids, her throat. And all the time she was crying and rocking with him, her head on his shoulder, her face pressed into his neck; it was there she first kissed him. He held away from her a little, and stroked her hair back again, and kissed her on the mouth. That made her cry more than ever, but she put up her face and kissed him, and now they were kissing each other, all wet and tangled, and her crying stopped, only that from time to time her whole body shook with a sob, making him kiss her more and more tenderly.

'I'm so cold!' were her first words.

'I'll get another blanket.' He got his legs from under him, numb after kneeling for so long, fetched a second blanket and wrapped it round her.

'I'll make a hot drink,' he said.

'The matches are beside the Primus.' Rose was not so far gone but that she fancied a hot drink, and this encouraged him.

'I'll light the fire first.' He struck a match and the kindling flared up, ready laid on the ash-pile under the logs.

The flare lit up Rose's face; she had turned on her front and was watching him, propped on her elbows. He balanced the kettle near the fierce heat of the fire and before long it was hot enough to pour on the spoonfuls of drinking chocolate and dried milk in the two mugs.

After a while he asked: 'What happened? Or would you rather not say?'

Her tears began afresh; but this time Chris did not move closer. He was not sure what would happen if he did, or if he could control himself, for his feelings had been aroused by their kisses.

He waited.

She had stayed for Nick till everyone had gone, not minding at first.

'He'd gone to put the petrol can back. But he might have thought of something else to do. Nick's like that – as you said, he does what he wants to do, whatever comes into his head.'

Touched yet pained by her resignation, Chris thought savagely: And what did you think he might be doing? Climbing trees? Playing in the tree-house? He asked, 'Why didn't you go after him?'

'I liked being there, waiting. It was so beautiful and peaceful after the boats had gone, with the moon getting up. Knowing he'd come back.'

'But he didn't?'

'No. So I went to Otter Lodge. I remembered I still had the key, to lock up. I heard him and Mrs Trewin talking, Jago was there too. I didn't hear what they were saying, they were walking away up the track towards Mirren Farm.' She put down her mug.

'Anyhow, you still thought he'd come back?'

She nodded. 'I thought he'd just walk up with them as far as Mirren – they must have come over by car. I got a bit fed up. I thought I'd give him a scare – hide in Otter Lodge and let him get back to the quay and not find me there. I waited and waited . . . I didn't want to go back by myself. It got awfully dark.'

'And you'd have had to go past the dead seamen – the Lascars.'

'That – yes. I suppose so. I just felt that if Nick wasn't coming back Otter Lodge was the only safe place to be.'

'Are you sure he knew you were waiting for him?'

'Oh, yes. I told him we'd sail back together – that it was our last night.'

'When?'

'Just before he did that fantastic thing, setting fire to the water.'

'Did you know he was absolutely pissed? He can drink a lot without showing it. And if he did hear you he must have forgotten. Yes, that was it, Rose, believe me. Drink makes you forget things.'

She seemed not to have heard him, but to be speaking her own thoughts aloud: 'He didn't want me mixed up with her. He never said anything, but I could feel that he didn't. Nick liked being with me, specially when we were sailing. He didn't have to worry about anything – he said so once when we were out in the bay. I didn't make demands on him, he said. So I tried not to. Mrs Trewin was different.'

'You knew, then?'

'That he stays the night there sometimes? Yes, I knew.' Her quiescent acceptance shocked him. It was worse than tears.

'I didn't for certain till a night or two ago. He'd walked home with me as far as the fence and we said goodnight. But I waited; and saw him take the moorland track to Trewin House. But I knew already, more or less, I could feel there was something. He'd look at me sometimes . . .

Oh, I don't know, as though he was sorry – no, not that – as though he was in a muddle and didn't know what to do. We'd be having fun –'

'What kind of fun?' Chris was surprised by jealousy.

She looked at him questioningly: 'The kind of fun you have on holiday.'

'I don't know. Did he kiss you?'

'Sometimes. But hardly at all, lately. He could see I was serious – yes, I think that was it. Why he stopped. What I thought was perhaps he was getting serious too, and was waiting for me to grow up a bit. Only two or three years' time – not long. Then we could be married.' She held out her hands to the embers. 'But waiting here, I saw it would never happen. His going off like that on our last night – it showed I wasn't important.

'I've wanted to talk about Nick, and Mrs Trewin. I thought it would help. But it makes me feel worse.' She put both hands under the blankets and pressed her belly.

'You could talk to Rowan?'

'Not much. She knew what I was feeling; but talking about it to her wouldn't have been any good. I thought you might understand about Nick – might explain things.'

'You think I know more about Nick than I do. Just being his kid brother doesn't . . .'

'People think that because you're young you don't – but you do – you feel just as much as older people – more, because . . .'

She had begun to shake all over. We ought to stop talking, he thought. Nothing can come of it.

'You're cold,' he said.

'My feet are terribly cold.'

'I'll warm them.' He kicked off his shoes and slipped down beside her inside the blankets.

'They're like ice.' He held her close to stop her shivering. She put her arms round his waist and rocked to dull the pain, and he felt her pain in him, and cared for nothing but to stop it if he could. And presently the pain turned to pleasure for them both.

When they woke it was light. Chris folded the blankets while Rose ran her fingers through her long hair. They locked up.

Going back, towing Mog's boat, the rising wind whipped the water into white waves. Neither of them had pullovers. But Chris did not like to move closer to Rose at the tiller, or put his arm round her for warmth, because he did not know how he stood with Rose or how he felt himself.

After all, it was he and not Nick who had made love to her, though it had come about almost by accident. He must not, he felt, take advantage of this, which was what led him to say, as they turned in to the hard, 'I don't suppose we shall see each other again.'

'No. I don't suppose we shall.'

'Besides,' he went on as though something unspoken had passed between them, 'you were thinking about Nick all the time, weren't you?'

As she brought *Seamouse* alongside, with extreme care not to scrape the varnish, a faint blush travelled from her neck to her hair-line. 'Not quite all the time,' she said.

Chris stood ankle-deep on the hard, feeling its roughness for the last time under his bare soles, watching *Seamouse* curve out into the main channel.

Walking up to the cottage he thought over some of what Rose had said. Extraordinary, her understanding of Nick, her acceptance of – well, almost anything that might happen in life. But then Rose, he now saw, was an extraordinary girl. They had talked together as he and Rowan could never have talked. He saw, too, what Nick meant when he spoke of Rowan belonging to the place, she and Danny together. He might want to return, but not to take Rowan away.

Nick must have got back first, for the door was bolted. Chris easily shinned up a gutter-pipe and squeezed through the small sash window.

Roused by their mother two hours later Chris asked, 'Did you go back for Rose?' He had to be certain.

'Yes. But how did you know?'

'I didn't. But I guessed you would.'

'Better change those filthy jeans.' Nick was stuffing his duffel-bag. 'She'd gone, not surprisingly.'

Chris believed him. He could easily have missed Mog's boat in darkness on the mud under the ten-foot quayside.

Nick gave Chris a thoughtful look; then, without another word, turned back to his packing.

No one at the cottages was awake to wave them goodbye. Indeed, Chris, squeezed in beside his mother on the back seat, knees to one side of the bucket seat in front, would have had a struggle to raise an arm.

As they bumped over the moor he squinted sideways to catch a last glimpse of Trewin House, its tall chimney like a finger, white as a swan against the grey sky, keeping vigil over the ships in their comings and goings. Dazed with sleeplessness, Chris's mind was a muddle of confused memories; the past fortnight was already distant, a little unreal. Only one feeling became clear: an urgent need to see Rose again as soon as possible, though how this was to be managed was too tiring to think about.

They had reached the main road and Nick had got out to open the gate when the familiar sound of drumming hooves reached them.

Chris, craning forward over the tip-up seat, saw Rowan, at a distance on a rounded hillock, rein in Snapdragon.

The Mitchells waved. She took off her Stetson hat and waved back.

Easing himself back in his corner, Chris thought: I shall get back somehow, some time.

EPILOGUE
1976

Chris stood at the gate of Mirren Farm, leaning his heavy knapsack against the gatepost, waiting for his children to catch him up. The early morning sun, through rafts of cloud, turned the steep meadows to gold, casting long shadows down towards the woods and the river.

'Come on!' he shouted, striding through the dewy grass, beginning to green over again after the drought. He was irritable after the long drive, and somehow nervy, as though the place they were making for might no longer exist – at least not as he remembered it after nearly twenty years.

Behind him, Anne complained, 'My sandals are squelching!'

Peter answered, 'Take them off, then. There – isn't it super? This may be the only place in all England, I shouldn't wonder, where you can walk through the dew in bare feet. Think of all those fields we went through – brown as toast.'

Coming to the gap in the fence, Chris swung his leg over the wire. Suddenly, in the thick woods, they were in half-darkness. Shafts of spidery light lit on creepers, ferns, webs spun from branch to branch, giant fungi wedged into twisted trunks.

'I don't like this place,' Anne said, 'it's witchy. Why couldn't we go with Mummy and Helen?' Helen was the baby.

'Because it was too early,' Pete answered with restraint, 'too early to wake people up. She had to get the key and fetch the boat. And we had to come on here and see the farmer and leave the car.' Then, raising his voice: 'And if you ask that boring question just one more time I'll thump you!'

Stumbling on hidden tree roots, tripped by brambles, slithering on mud layered with rotting leaves, Chris, with his usual pessimism, thought, what a way to begin a holiday! He remembered his brother Nick saying, 'Never go back to a place where you've been happy. It never works a second time.'

At the moment when Chris was certain he had missed the path and must admit it, they came out on a clearing and a low wooden house with the river beyond.

'Otter Lodge,' he said, swinging the pack off his back. The little house was screened by trees from the river; but westwards the view opened on the upper reaches, trees trailing branches in the water, stubble fields on the far bank that caught the light. With the increase of the sun's heat mist coiled off the river, and patches of sun on the still waters reflected intense light that hurt Chris's eyes, strained by hours of driving through the night.

'Gosh!' murmured Pete. 'Oh, glory! What an absolutely super place!'

Anne was peering through the half-glass doors. 'There are bunks, and cooking things, and stacks of logs. Oh, and a hat hanging on the wall – a cowboy's hat.'

Pete had climbed down over the rocks. 'Come and look at this!'

The two children began to explore. Chris unrolled a groundsheet on the heather. They had slept all night in the van: he had been awake for most of it. But his was not unpleasant tiredness. A delicious langour stole over him as he stretched out, and all the cares and tensions of life began to slip away, like the mist off the river. It was what Danny and Rowan had done for him, years back. It was like coming home. He thought of the hat on the wall. The Stetson hat!

He had the clearest memory of Rowan astride *Snapdragon*, waving. She had married a local man, just as Nick had said she should.

And he, Chris . . . he vaguely recollected a talk with

Mog: 'D'you ever feel you're being rail-roaded through life?' That feeling, had he foreseen it, was to continue almost until this moment. School, teacher-training, early marriage, kids. Years abroad. Good years, full years. But he was glad to be back in his own country.

'The very first holiday we have in England,' he had promised his wife, 'I'll take you to Otter Lodge.'

'We've found a tree-house!' Anne stood over him. 'It's super – ever so big and high up.'

'Keep away from it, it's sure to be unsafe. Rotten, after so many years. Keep away, *I mean that.*' He sat up.

'It's not,' Pete came up. 'The ladder's been mended. And you can see new wood – proper tonguing-and-grooving.'

The tree-house was just as he remembered it, and newly repaired. Danny, I bet, he thought with affection.

'O.K.,' he climbed down, 'but for all our sakes don't fall out and spoil the holiday.'

There was no need: seven-year-old Anne climbed up, sure-footed as her uncle Nick. And Pete cautious, like himself. Even at eleven, he thought, you can see he'll be like me – like I was then. A bit dreamy, going for what I wanted, ignoring whole chunks of life going on around me. All those Travises, those "cousins". He smiled at the memory. Don't suppose I ever got to know one from t'other, not properly, except Mog. And Tosh, perhaps.

Hadn't he been a bit young for his age in some ways, even for those days? Mrs Trewin had shown she thought so. *She* was an oddball. Never stayed the same. Never sized her up. But maybe no one could, not even Jago. You had to take her as she was. And Nick, he supposed, had done just that.

Nick . . . a partner in his brewery, twice married, four kids. More "cousins"!

'Dad!' Pete was shouting from the tree-house, 'there's a boat coming up the river. I bet it's Mum!'

'About time.' And as the children ran past him: 'Here – this way! Here's where the boat will come in.'

He led them through the ash grove down to the little harbour. He looked downstream, recalling every detail. watching the curve of the river where it divided.

And there, sure enough, standing at the tiller, and with a carrycot balanced across the thwart, came Rose.